Victorian Splendor

EVEN MORE EMBROIDERY AND PASTIMES

FOR THE 21ST CENTURY

For Ron, Mary and Sue Gray,
my family and my friends—at last.

First published in 2001
by Quilters' Resource Inc.
P.O. Box 148850
Chicago, IL 60614
Phone 773 278-5695

Designer: Suzy King
Photography: Simon Blackall
Styling: Jenny Haskins
Technical quilt block photography: Andrew Payne, Photographix
Printed and bound in China

Library of Congress
Cataloguing-in-Publication Data

Haskins, Jenny
Victorian Splendor : even more embroidery and pastimes for the 21st century
ISBN 1 - 889682 - 15 - 9

Jenny Haskins

Victorian Splendor

EVEN MORE EMBROIDERY AND PASTIMES FOR THE 21ST CENTURY

Quilters' Resource publications

INTRODUCTION

8

GENERAL
SEWING REQUIREMENTS

10

VICTORIAN LACE
EMBROIDERY BY MACHINE

12

A BANQUET OF
INDULGENT COLOR

16

VICTORIAN TRIVIA
LADY JOSEPHINE, FANTASIA FAN

18

CASCADING BLOSSOMS

25

FANCIFUL
LITTLE PURSES

26

ROMANTIC NET WRAP

29

VICTORIAN NET SKIRT

31

GLAMOROUS
EVENING BODICE

32

MAGNIFICENT
OBSESSION QUILT

34

Contents

BETHANY DOLL

44

PIANO SHAWL

50

ROMANTIC ROSE
TABLE QUILT

54

VICTORIAN HIGH TEA
TABLECLOTH

56

LACE CURTAIN

62

LACE TRIMMED
LINEN

64

SPLENDOR IN
LINEN AND LACE

68

GLORIA'S
FRAMED LADIES

92

LAVISH
LACE FAN

96

PICTURE
OF ELEGANCE

99

TECHNIQUES
OF SPLENDOR

100

CREDITS

103

Introduction

Simon and Diane, my partners in the Victorian Trilogy, first *Victorian Pansies*, then *Victorian Roses* and now *Victorian Splendor*, have both played a part in the production of these books. Turn the pages and you can catch a glimpse of each of us. Simon captures the essence of each project with his use of natural light in his magnificent photography, Diane attends to editing details and makes sure all the instructions hang together and me—well I love color and being creative with it. Each of us brings strengths to a team that exists for the production of these books. Working long hours and weekends seems natural to bring together projects that delight the eye and excite the soul. I aim for beauty in color, fabric and thread through the medium of the magnificent PFAFF sewing machines and the results are projects designed for all levels of sewing skill and artistic endeavor.

As promised in *Victorian Roses*, the design CD Victorian Lace, has been produced, replicating handmade lace from my antique lace collection, and *Victorian Splendor* utilizes these magic designs along with Victorian Pansies and my butterfly disk and of course, the accompanying CD, Victorian Piano Shawl. This is the first book (that we are aware of) that includes a design CD. And the disk contains all the designs from an original Victorian piano shawl.

I have called upon my talented friends and fellow artists to participate in this feast of color and design. Gloria McKinnon, who has supported me

from the start along with her team from Anne's Glory Box, Carole Cree from Flights of Fancy, Wendy Fenwick, doll maker and machine artist, the team from Sharman's sewing center, magic ladies with exceptional talent, Judy Wearne, heirloom specialist from the Heirloom Studio and Jane Nesbitt Educational Director for Pfaff Sewing Machines. Closer to home, Lucie and Elaine have assisted me in all areas whether test stitching designs, making the project or just being there. It has been my delight to see these talented artists perform their magic with thread, fabric and embroidery.

I would also like to thank my family, who are always there for me, especially my beautiful daughter Sam, who has always believed in me and is my 'keeper'. As she once said to the immigration officer at LA airport when asked what she did, she replied, 'I make sure she eats and sleeps'. Thanks also to Simon my son, who is a free spirit along with Jason, my eldest son who is discovering what it means to believe in yourself.

I am dedicating this book to my parents Ron and Mary Gray, who are now in their late eighties, amazing people who have lived their lives in the belief that through God all things are possible and my sister Sue, who has come of age believing in herself and the power of love. I bear witness to the fact that my gifts come through me and not of me and therefore all praise goes to the Creator.

With the advent of the Pfaff 2140 the creative possibilities of machine embroidery are stretched beyond present day horizons.

Victorian Splendor gives you the inspiration to use the Pfaff sewing machines to make your dreams realities creating heirlooms from the past for the future.

Jenny Haskins

- *Pfaff embroidery machine 7560, 7570 or 2140 with Creative Fantasy Embroidery Unit*
- *Pfaff PC-Designer Software*
- *Pfaff Creative Card Station*
- *Pfaff Creative blank memory cards*
- *Pfaff Victorian Lace CD by Jenny Haskins*
- *Victorian Roses CD by Jenny Haskins*
- *Victorian Piano Shawl CD by Jenny Haskins which accompanies this book*
- *MACHINE FEET: open-toe foot, normal sewing foot, ¼-inch foot, zipper foot, narrow edge foot, clear-view freehand foot, 7-groove pin tucking foot and cording blade and 6mm pin tucking foot*
- *MACHINE NEEDLES: size-80 embroidery needle, size-75 universal needle, size-60 sharp, 1.6/70 twin needle, 2.5/80 twin needle and size-120 wing needle*
- *Madeira pre-wound bobbins*
- *Madeira rayon 40 embroidery thread*
- *Madeira Cotona 50 heirloom cotton thread*
- *Monofilament thread*
- *Madeira gold metallic thread*
- *Self-adhesive tear-away stabilizer/Filmoplast*
- *Romeo water soluble stabilizer*
- *Melt-away stabilizer*
- *Photocopy paper for stabilizer*
- *Vliesofix/Wonderunder double-sided fusible web*
- *Hobb's Ultra-thin Thermore batting for machine quilting*
- *Fusible batting*
- *Fabric marking pens, both water and air fading*
- *Chalk pencil*
- *Vellum (112gsm) tracing paper to print out placement templates*
- *Self-healing cutting mat, quilting ruler and rotary cutter*
- *Protractor for exact angles*
- *Scissors, dressmaking, paper and small sharp*
- *Tape measure and ruler*
- *Hand-painted rayon laces*
- *Jenny Haskins Victorian Prints*
- *Pins, both lace and quilting*
- *Hand embroidery, sewing and beading needles*

VICTORIAN LACE
By machine

Victorian Lace or lace of any type—its beauty, intricate pattern details and the wonder of its gossamer threads—has been a passion of mine for as long as I can remember.

From the moment I was introduced to Pfaff machines and their amazing ability to produce machine embroidery I was fascinated by the possibilities their wonderful stitches presented. The result, published in 1992, was my book *Victorian Dreams, The Creative Art of Lace Making by Machine* using the Pfaff 1475 sewing machine. In it I documented the creation of lace using the built-in stitches, sewn out in rows over cotton net tulle, now known as 'stitch building'.

Even though time consuming, the results were amazing and opened the door to lace making by machine using available stitches and stitches modified by or created with the software. By today's standards it all seems very primitive, but it was revolutionary then when Pfaff was the first and only sewing machine to interface with a computer and create stitches using the PC-Designer software.

It has always been a dream of mine to be able to use and share my wonderful antique lace collection—and still keep the originals. You can imagine how hard it is to cut into 100-year-old lace without feeling a twinge of guilt, especially when thinking of the thousands of hours it took to make, probably by candlelight.

When Pfaff approached me to do the designs for a CD, there was no second choice—it had to be Victorian lace from my antique collection. The results are spectacular, the digitizing is superb and the creative possibilities are endless. *Victorian Splendor* is the result of my first creative ventures using these amazing lace designs. I know this is just the tip of the 'laceberg' and cannot wait to explore more creative variations and computations.

The secret to any embroidery is to know how to make the process simple and achievable; the trick is using the correct products to get a perfect and professional result. The following information should act as a guide for the novice as well as the experienced sewer when using the Victorian Lace CD to sew antique lace by machine.

NOTE: *The instructions that come with Victorian Lace are excellent so if all else fails, read the instructions.*

WHY A COMPACT DISK?

Technology is moving fast and always presenting better ways of doing things. CDs are lightweight, durable and cheap, and a CD's memory capacity is much greater than a floppy disk or memory card. The lace designs are so large in stitch count (memory intense) that you would need several floppy disks and many cards to store them. You will notice this as you may only get one design on a Pfaff Creative memory card such as 20a and 20b [file (1) and (2)].

Storing designs on a CD allows the sewer to access the designs on the computer using the PC-Designer software in order to modify and combine the designs when possible. The software also allows the sewer to print out the designs as they come on the CD (or those you have modified and created) on vellum (112gsm) tracing paper to act as a template for perfect placement on your fabric or stabilizer.

USING VELLUM (112GSM) TRACING PAPER TEMPLATES

1 Print out the chosen design using the 1.1 ratio setting in the format options (the design will print exactly the size of the embroidery) on the tracing paper. Feed tracing paper through one sheet at a time if your printer tends to take several sheets at once.

2 On the printout draw a horizontal and a vertical line through the center of the design (marked with a small cross) and extend them both to the outer hoop line.

3 Using a sharp point such as the end of a pair of small scissors, make a small hole in the center (marked with a cross) and at each end of the lines.

4 Place the template on the fabric in the required position and direction, then use a water or air fading fabric-marking pen to mark through the holes punched in the template onto the fabric.

5 Remove template and use a ruler and the fabric-marking pen to connect the marked points with lines—these will be aligned later with the corresponding marks (notches) on the hoop to ensure perfect placement. Mark with an arrowhead the direction the design should face. Also find and mark the starting position of the design on the fabric.

Place the hoop in the sewing machine then use the lines and direction arrow on the fabric to position the fabric over the self-adhesive stabilizer, matching your drawn lines with the marks (notches) on the hoop and placing the center intersection directly under the needle. In the case of hooped fabric, you will hoop the fabric and match drawn lines with hoop marks (notches) prior to attaching the hoop to the machine.

Press pattern start and the needle swings to the starting position of the design—directly over the starting position marked on the fabric.

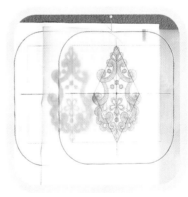

You will find the templates valuable tools for accurate placement when positioning connecting designs. Place template on fabric in desired position, aligning with previously embroidered design, and transfer all markings through to the fabric before embroidering your second design. Repeat the process for mutliples of the same design.

PLACEMENT JUMP STITCHES

1 Each of the lace designs on Victorian Lace has long placement jump stitches that extend to the design extremities. On the template make holes at these extremities, place template over fabric, mark fabric through holes as before, remove the template and connect the dots for marked placement lines.

2 These jump stitches are always 'color 1' of the design and when stitched on the fabric should exactly sit over the marked placement lines on the fabric to ensure accurate embroidery placement. Refer to the insert in Victorian Lace for detailed directions on the use of these positioning stitches for connecting different designs and for stitching multiples of the same design.

STABILIZER

✿ For embroidery on fabric where the back cannot be seen or is not to be seen, use the self-adhesive tear-away technique in *Victorian Pansies* (refer to Techniques Directory on page 100 of this book).

NOTE: *All stabilizers can be sprayed with a quilt basting spray so they become self-adhesive. Fabric placed over the sprayed-on surface of the stabilizer adheres to it and this is referred to in the text as the 'stick-and-sew technique'. Remove stablilizer after embroidering by tearing away, ironing or washing.*

✿ Water soluble stabilizers such as Romeo are excellent for stand-alone designs. Stitch out the design over several layers of stabilizer, remove the stabilizer from the hoop, cut away as much excess stabilizer from around the design as possible then soak the embroidery in hot water for at least 30 minutes, wash in warm soapy water and rinse until the water is clear and all stabilizer has been removed. You may need to boil the embroidery to remove every trace of stabilizer to leave your embroidery soft.

✿ Stand-alone designs on Victorian Lace that can be stitched over a water-soluble stabilizer only are: Lace1, Lace2, Lace3, Lace6, Lace7, Lace12, Lace13, Lace14, Lace16 Lace17, Lace18, Lace19c and Lace19b.

✿ Lace designs that connect to form a continuous line are: Lace14, Lace19, Lace19c Lace 19b, Lace20a and Lace20b (stitched in the large hoop to form one design, which has a connecting point to make into a continuous line). Lace9 and Lace10 (Lace 9 sits above and is 'cradled' by Lace10) can also be stitched in a continuous line which is composed of two separate lace designs whose shapes are complementary

✿ When you make lace-edged fabric on voile or cotton net tulle, part of the lace design will stand alone. Use water soluble Romeo plus basting spray beneath the fine fabric, stitch the lace, remove Romeo by washing as before then carefully cut around the outside edge of the lace.

✿ Melt-away stabilizer, a type of plastic film, has a rough side which sits against the fabric to prevent slipping. It is placed in the hoop and treated as you would a water-soluble stabilizer. Instead of removing the stabilizer with water, use a hot steam iron to remove the stabilizer from the back of the embroidery. The stabilizer melts and the residue is removed from the iron by wiping with a damp cloth. This is ideal in heirloom sewing for transparent fabrics that you do not want to wash.

THREADS

These lace designs are very dense so never use a thread heavier than a 40 denier. Heirloom and metallic threads also stitch out beautifully.

✿ For best results use: Madeira rayon 40 embroidery thread, metallic thread, or Cotona heirloom thread, either 50 or 80 denier.

✿ Rayon thread dyes well so use left-over threads in similar colors (such as creams) to stitch out lace designs then dye them using the antique dyeing technique found in *Victorian Pansies* (see page 100 in the Techniques Directory of this book).

BOBBINS

I use Madeira pre-wound bobbins for all my embroidery. This is especially important for fine fabrics and lace embroidery designs as the bobbin thread is very fine and soft and helps keep your embroidery soft, reducing the bulk at the back.

NEEDLES

I usually use a size-80 embroidery needle as it has a large eye. In some cases I will use a size-80 topstitch needle that has an even larger eye.

COLOR, FABRIC AND THREAD

Color is that magic ingredient that sets my head on fire, my heart pumping and my creativity soaring; it is exciting, contagious and intoxicating. Purple, my own favorite color, acts like a magnet on my senses and I never tire of it. Finding new ways to use it is a source of endless fascination for me.

They say 'color my world', well color fills my creative world and once I have seen a new color or color combination then straightaway it has to be interpreted with thread and fabric or in some other facet of design.

There is no doubt that 'color sense' is a gift. I'm hopeless with numbers or names, but color, well that's another story because I do have an excellent color memory and can exactly match fabric, thread, lace or ribbon with ease after seeing a color briefly, and just once. It is a God-given gift as are all my talents, but a particularly valuable one as it is the color that either makes or breaks your embroidery.

I cannot work in a space that is not harmoniously color coordinated. I did an interior decorating course once and we were lectured on the physiological effect color has on our lives and the way we react to color. Some colors are soothing, some stimulating to our senses, some are pleasing and some are not, but in one way or another everyone reacts to color. A technically correct, well-executed design can be ruined by bad color choices, whereas the reverse applies in a poorly executed design which has wonderful color because the inadequate sewing skills can be overlooked.

There is no need to struggle with color. Choose wisely and well and soon you will be an expert. Select a fabric that you just adore, then take it into a sewing store and choose the threads that exactly match the fabric and you cannot go wrong. Remember 'less is best' so do not use any more that five different colors for one project and repeat the colors in different ways and sequences.

Lay out your fabric, threads, and trims, placing them where you will walk past them every day in the house, and live with them. If a color offends, remove it. Employ the old adage 'if in doubt leave it out' and this way you can be assured of success with color.

Be aware also of your favorite color as this is your 'color comfort zone' and you will be drawn to using shades of this color. My color comfort zone is purple.

A BANQUET OF
Indulgent Color

It's a majestic color that demands attention; maybe it reflects who I am—some would say so anyway! I also like colors that are muted such as antique gold and warm green with either gray or black added to the color to give it an old, rich look that is perhaps more subtle.

With cool and warm colors, never mix the two unless intending to achieve a particular effect. Many a time I have seen a wonderful piece of art ruined by one color—even the smallest amount of the wrong color can make a big difference.

The use of a shading and reducing glass is a vital aid to the correct balance of color and design. You need to 'shrink' a design to see its imperfections and this is what a reducing glass does; reduces the designs elements down to a manageable picture so you can evaluate the balance of color and design. The shading glass converts all colors to shades of one color only so the artist can gauge the balance of light and dark tones in a large work such as a quilt or a wall hanging.

It is always possible to dye threads, especially rayon threads, or tone them down with such dyes as potassium permanganate, a technique covered in *Victorian Pansies* (see Techniques Directory on page 100 of this book). You can do this before or after embroidery. Tea and coffee dyes also work well, but I prefer the potassium permanganate technique.

When working with colors, fear is limiting; the fear of what others will say or think or the nagging doubts about whether or not the colors, fabrics, threads and embellishments will work can hold you back. I know I was like that for years when contemplating the use of purple—everyone gave me a hard time over purple but now I use it with complete abandon and some of my most popular works are in purple.

So go to 'courage' (a place less populated than 'timidity'), rid yourself of fear, give yourself permission to be free thus setting your creativity loose and I promise you, you will be amazed at the results. Believe in yourself and all things are absolutely possible—I am living proof of this. 'Life is a banquet table, at which most poor fools are sitting starving' said Aunty Mame to her nephew, Patrick, so I am inviting you to feast at the table of life and enjoy the banquet (of color in this case).

VICTORIAN
Trivia

*Knick knacks from the Victorian era continue to intrigue us.
The half doll, embroidered fan and embroidered lace neck purse
are highly decorative objects which are quick to make
and have become favorite projects in my
classses and seminars.*

LADY
Josephine

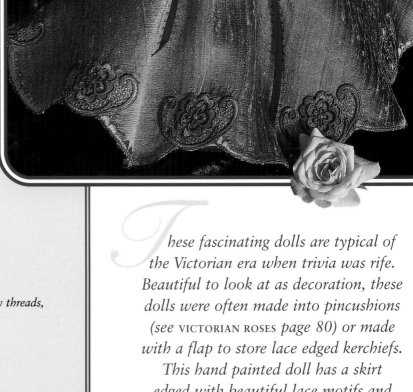

MATERIALS

- 12cm (3¾in) Victorian porcelain half-doll
- 48cm x 38cm (19in x 15in) rectangle suitable fabric such as silk dupione, moire taffeta or satin for skirt
- 60cm (24in) narrow satin ribbon for tying
- 10cm (4in) beaded fringe
- Small trinket or button
- Sheet of heavyweight vellum (112gsm) tracing paper
- Pfaff Victorian Lace CD
- Pfaff PC-Designer software
- Pfaff Creative memory card
- Machine needle: size-80 top stitch needle
- Machine feet: open-toe embroidery foot
- THREADS: Madeira rayon 40 embroidery threads, dark and light pink or colors to suit
- Madeira pre-wound bobbins
- Self-adhesive tear-away
- Photocopy paper for stabilizer
- 450 craft glue
- Glitter glue
- Hand sewing needle and thread
- Tracing paper, paper scissors and lead pencil
- General sewing requirements

These fascinating dolls are typical of the Victorian era when trivia was rife. Beautiful to look at as decoration, these dolls were often made into pincushions (see VICTORIAN ROSES *page 80) or made with a flap to store lace edged kerchiefs. This hand painted doll has a skirt edged with beautiful lace motifs and built-in stitches.*

PREPARATION

1 Use the tracing paper and lead pencil to trace the skirt pattern from the pattern sheet making sure you trace all the lines and embroidery placement details. Use the fabric-marking pen to transfer this pattern to the fabric for the skirt. Mark all lines, embroidery positions and scalloped hem but **DO NOT CUT OUT**.

EMBROIDERY

LACE MOTIF EMBROIDERY

Use the Pfaff PC-Designer software, blank card and the Victorian Lace CD to transfer Lace19a to the blank card for embroidery.

2 Use self-adhesive tear-away in the hoop as a stabilizer, size-80 machine needle and a pre-wound bobbin. Select two shades of pink that best match those used to embroider Lace19a on the positions marked around the skirt, starting at the center back seam. Embroider seven designs around the bottom of the skirt in the positions marked.

3 Join the center back seam with a narrow French seam and press then embroider the eighth design centered over the seam.

BUILT-IN STITCH EMBROIDERY

4 Use the open-toe embroidery foot, size-80 top stitch needle, pre-wound bobbin, rayon 40 embroidery threads and photocopy paper as stabilizer to embroider around the scallops that connect the lace embroidery at the bottom of the skirt.

5 Use threads that best match those used to embroider stitch No 60, width and length 6.0, density 0.25, straight edge following the drawn scallop. You may need to mirror this stitch depending on the direction in which you are sewing. On the outside of this stitch on the straight edge, sew stitch No 16, width 1.5, length 0.6 using the darker pink thread.

PUTTING IT TOGETHER

6 Press the lower edge of the skirt from the wrong side of the embroidery then use a small sharp pair of scissors to cut around the embroidery on the bottom edge of the skirt and center circle to fit waist of doll.

7 Use the glitter glue to simulate beads and place a small dot in the center of the flower in each lace embroidery and at the top of each embroidered scallop around the bottom of the hem—allow to dry thoroughly before proceeding.

8 Use the hand-sewing needle and double thread to slightly gather up the top of the skirt to fit the waist of the half doll.

9 Place the skirt over the doll, pull up to fit the waist of the doll, and secure with a triple knot. Use the 450 glue to secure the skirt in place.

10 Glue the beaded fringe over the gathers at the top of the skirt then use the narrow ribbon to tie around the waist of the doll covering the beaded ribbon and finish with a bow.

11 Glue the small trinket in place over the bow as an added optional decoration.

12 To make the cone shape that supports the doll:

—trace the skirt pattern as supplied (half the fabric skirt) onto the heavy vellum tracing paper finishing at the 4cm (1⅝in) positioning straight line.

—use the paper scissors to cut this out (do not cut out for waist)

—roll into a cone, overlapping the seam allowance and secure with glue

13 Insert the pointed end of the cone inside the half doll and secure with glue—this allows the doll to be free standing and supports the skirt.

You may wish to place the doll over a special bottle of perfume or use her to secrete that special something that only you know about. These dolls make beautiful gifts and look wonderful on a dressing table or windowsill.

*A*part from looking brilliant, this fan is fun to make and is an excellent teaching tool. Use the Pfaff large hoop for stitch building and instead of hand beading, add time-saving glitter glue to the embroidery.

MATERIALS

- 34cm x 150cm (13⅜in x 60in) strip fabric for fan
- 61cm x 30cm (24in x 11½in) iron-on batting for fan
- 25cm x 30cm (10in x 12in) fringing for tassel
- 8cm (3¼in) beaded fringe for tassel
- 61cm x 6mm (24in x ¼in) ribbon for fan
- Small charm or button
- Sheet of medium weight cardboard 62cm x 51cm (25in x 20in)
- 3.45m x 1cm (3¾yd x ⅜in) edging lace
- Six lace flowers
- Glitter glue for simulated beads
- Long fine needle and strong thread
- 450 craft glue
- Helmar's quilt basting spray
- Pfaff Victorian Lace CD
- Pfaff blank card
- Pfaff PC-Designer software
- Pfaff large hoop
- THREADS: Madeira rayon 40 in rose pink, olive green, dark grape and metallic gold
- Madeira pre-wound bobbins
- MACHINE FEET: open-toe foot and clear-view freehand foot
- Machine needles: size-80 top stitch needle
- Vellum (112gsm) tracing paper
- Self-adhesive tear-away stabilizer
- Photocopy paper for stabilizer
- Lead pencil and paper scissors to trace and cut out cardboard/Vellum
- General sewing requirements

PREPARATION

1 Use the lead pencil and the tracing paper to trace around the fan template from the pattern sheet then cut it out accurately to be used as a template.

2 Use the fabric-marking pen and the template on the pattern sheet to trace around then cut out in:

—lightweight cardboard—10 segments front and back of fan then use the hole punch to punch a hole in the bottom of each segment

—fusible batting—five segments for front of fan

—fan fabric allowing a 1cm (⅜in) seam allowance on all sides beyond the fabric-marking pen lines which will be on the wrong side of the fabric, 10 segments in all for front and back of fan. It is advisable to cut five of these segments for the front out roughly first giving extra fabric to allow for embroidery, then redraw template outline on wrong side of fabric when embroidery is completed before cutting out accurately around the seam allowance.

3 Lightly spray five fan segments (back) with basting spray (see tip page 39), then center the five accurately cut-out fabric segments over the cardboard segments, making sure the fabric is flat and smooth with the traced lines on fabric matching the cardboard edges.

4 Clip into and around the curves on the fabric, making sure these clips end just outside the cardboard template edges. Place one covered fan segment on a flat clean surface with the cardboard side uppermost.

5 Apply the 450 glue to the outside edge of the cardboard template, allow to set for a few minutes then pull the fabric over the glue so it follows the shape of the template and sits flat and smooth from the right side. Repeat for remaining four segments.

6 Use the 450 glue to apply the straight side of the edging lace around the edge of the above segments, clipping the lace so it sits flat around the scalloped edges at the top and the narrow curved end of each strut. Have the lace scallops facing out with the right side of the lace uppermost. Set all five segments to one side.

7 On two of the fabric pieces to be embroidered, center the fusible batting, rough side to back of fabric, aligning the traced lines with edge of batting, then iron in place with a hot steam iron.

8 Use the fabric-marking pen, ruler and the template to mark the embroidery lines on the above fan segments.

9 Use the fabric-marking pen, ruler and the template to mark the center vertical and horizontal lines of the remaining roughly cut out pieces of fabric for embroidery motif positioning.

EMBROIDERY

All embroidery requires a size-80 top stitch needle and a Madeira pre-wound bobbin.

EMBROIDERY MOTIF

Use the Pfaff PC-Designer software, a blank card and the Pfaff Victorian Lace CD to download design 15a and 15b to a blank card.

10 Use threads that best match those used to embroider Lace15a and 15b using the Pfaff large hoop and the fabric segments that **DO NOT** have the

fusible batting ironed to them. Refer to page 100 for the use of the large hoop.

When embroidery is complete remove fabric from the self-adhesive tear-away and press.

Embroider three fan segments in this way then center the remaining three fusible batting templates (rough side to the wrong side of fabric) under the embroidery, making sure they match the template outline, then iron in place using a hot steam iron from the right side of the fabric.

11 Use the glitter glue pen to simulate beads by placing a small dot of glitter on each intersection of the two grids in the design, in the center of all the dots, across the arch at the bottom of the center spiral and around the edge of the three spirals at the top of the fan—remember less is best—then set aside to dry thoroughly.

BUILT-IN STITCH EMBROIDERY

All embroidery requires the open-toe foot and photocopy paper as stabilizer (at the back of the embroidery) as well as the Madeira pre-wound bobbins, rayon 40 thread and size 80 needle. Use the

23

remaining two fan segments that have the fusible batting ironed to the back of them.

12 Use threads that best match those used and the positioning lines to embroider the stitches starting with the center line, referring to the template on the pattern sheet for stitch numbers and sequence. Start and finish beyond the drawn template outline at the beginning and end of each row of stitching.

13 Complete embroidery with curved row of satin stitch balls to cover ends of simulated ribbon stitching.

FREEHAND STIPPLE QUILTING

14 Set up the machine for freehand stitching by placing the clear view freehand foot on the machine, lowering the feed dogs, slightly tightening the bobbin and loosening the upper tension.

15 Stipple quilting is a continuous meandering line that has no sharp angles and stitching lines never intersect one another. Use the gold metallic thread to stipple-quilt the fabric around the rows of machine embroidery.

PUTTING IT TOGETHER

16 Cover the front fan segments in the same manner as the backing segments, making sure that the embroidery designs are centered over the cardboard templates, then clip the fabric edges and glue in place from the back. Allow glue to dry completely.

17 Use topstitch No 1, stitch length 2.0 and needle positions to stitch close to the edge of each fan segment around the edge to complete the embroidery on all 10 segments.

18 You may also choose to embroider stitch No 165 width and length 4.0 density 0.25 around the top of each back segment following the curves on the top of the segment either before or after you have glued them to the cardboard—the Pfaff 'dual feed' system allows you to do this through the cardboard and fabric with ease.

19 From the cardboard side of each segment use the sharp end of a small pair of scissors to pierce the fabric at the bottom end of each strut through the previously punched hole.

20 On the wrong side, squeeze a line of 450 glue around the outside edge and in sections of the center of each fan segment, then place the backs to fronts, aligning the edges, and pin if necessary until glue is set.

21 Stack completed fan segments alternating motif embroidery with built-in stitch embroidery and aligning the holes. Use the long needle and heavy thread (doubled) to go through the holes at the bottom of each segment starting and finishing on one side, then secure with a decorative bead or button.

TO MAKE THE TASSEL

—take three strands of the fringe on the end that is to be in the center of the tassel (the end that is rolled first) and tie their ends in a triple knot

—apply glue to the top edge (braid section) of the fringe then roll up tightly

—find the triple knot, hold securely letting the fringe fall over the rolled-up edge

—loop knotted end of fringe over a door handle or such, or get someone to hold it for you

—make sure the fringe is evenly distributed over the rolled-up end, then secure with a cord below the rolled-up end with several cords taken from the fringe and finish with a triple knot to make a 'waist'

—glue the beaded fringe over the above, tie cords then cover the ribbon with a small piece of lace

22 Attach tassel to the bead or button that holds the fan segments together.

TO COMPLETE THE FAN

23 Turn the fan to the wrong side, so that the segments overlap evenly (only by a small amount) then place a dab of glue at the start and finish of the machine embroidery on the first segment and the finish only on the remaining four segments. Place the narrow ribbon across the back of the fan so that it sits firmly across each segment and is glued in place. Glue a small flower over each section of the ribbon that has glue under it. Also glue a flower at the base of the segment that is uppermost to cover the hole punched through the fabric. Allow to dry before opening and closing the fan. Do not glue the ribbon down all the way or the fan will not open and close.

NB: *Instructions for the embroidered lace neck purse are on the CD which accompanies this book.*

24

CASCADING
Blossoms

The central motif of Narelle Grieve's masterpiece quilt (displayed at the Houston Quilt Market and Festival, 2000) is hand embroidery cut from an antique kimono. During a creative morning tea with me she decided on a one branch design instead of a whole tree. Narelle specializes in intricate handwork, my medium is the sewing machine but we are both driven by a love of beauty and a fascination with fabrics and threads.

FANCIFUL
Little Purses

❧❧❧

*A touch of hand-painted machine-embroidered lace is added
to these delightful little purses along with beading and hand
embroidery, giving them a definite Victorian flair.
Whether your purse is old or new, the addition
of lace gives that special touch
that demands attention.*

ROMANTIC
Net Wrap

*Cotton net tulle is transformed as if by magic
into a romantic lace trimmed wrap, edged in beading
and sprinkled with lace butterflies—Cinderella would
be proud to wear this to a ball.*

- *1m (1⅛yd) cotton net tulle*
- *Romeo water-soluble stabilizer*
- *Helmar's quilt basting spray*
- *Pfaff Victorian Lace CD by Jenny Haskins*
- *Pfaff PC-Designer Software*
- *Pfaff Creative memory card*
- *Vellum (112gsm) tracing paper*
- *6 x 1000 meter reels of Madeira rayon 40 thread in shades of pale cream*
- *Madeira pre-wound bobbins*
- *MACHINE NEEDLE: size-80 embroidery needle*
- *MACHINE FEET: clear-view freehand foot*
- *22 amber beaded tassels*
- *Hand sewing needle and thread*
- *Water-soluble fabric-marking pen*
- *Potassium permanganate crystals to use as dye*
- *General sewing requirements.*

PREPARATION

1 Square the tulle, trim off excess then divide it in half on the diagonal to make two triangles. Put one aside for the wrap.

2 Cut strips of tulle 23cm (9in) wide the width of the fabric to be used for edge lace embroidery.

3 Use the PC-Designer software, Victorian Lace CD and a blank card to transfer Lace11, Lace12, Lace14, Lace14b and Lace16—these may not all fit on a memory card at one time.

4 Use the tracing paper and refer to page 12 for printing out and using placement templates to print out the above designs and mark the positioning holes.

EMBROIDERY

Use one layer of Romeo under the net tulle, a size-80 embroidery needle, Madeira rayon 40 embroidery thread and Madeira pre-wound bobbins for all embroidery.

NOTE: *Use up partly used reels of several shades of cream or beige thread for embroidery. When it is dyed, the slight variation in color will accent the aged look of the wrap.*

5 Refer to the method covered in step 14, page 75, for the embroidery of Lace14 in a continuous line and Lace14b singly, but done here on the cotton net tulle strips placed on the hoop over the Romeo (stick-and-sew technique, page 14). Nine designs are joined together on the two short sides of the triangle and 12 designs across the long side of the triangle with a single Lace14b for each of the three corners. Each design takes 55 minutes and 160m of thread so take your time and keep that sewing machine stitching.

6 When the embroidery is complete make sure you join any sections that need to be joined so they appear to be continuous then remove the stabilizer from the back of the embroidery by cutting away excess then refer to page 14 for the removal of Romeo from the embroidery.

7 Use a small sharp pair of scissors to cut around both edges of the lace close to the last row of stitching and cut between the satin stitched connecting bars on either side of the flower and between the leaves on each design.

8 Use the Vellum (112gsm) tracing paper templates and the photo as a guide to position Lace16 in each corner of the wrap and Lace11 and Lace12 (butterflies) scattered over the back of the wrap. Remove the soluble stabilizer as in step 6.

COMPLETING THE WRAP

Measure in 5cm (2in) from the cut edges and use a fabric marking pen and ruler to draw lines parallel to the edges of the wrap as guidelines for the edging lace.

9 Pin then baste the edging lace in place so the small connecting flower is centered over the guideline and the flower edge faces the center of the wrap. Position and pin nine designs down both short sides of the shawl. Position 12 designs across the long side of the triangle, clipping the lace if necessary at the corners, then place Lace14b in each of the sharply angled corners so it sits over the two flowers that are on either side of each corner and completes the edge. (The lace edge should form a continuous scallop, so make sure the corner edges match, then sew them together.)

10 Use the clear-view freehand foot and rayon 40 embroidery thread and a narrow zigzag stitch to freehand stitch the lace in place. Stitch around the 'flower' edge of the lace which faces the center of the wrap.

11 Use small sharp scissors to clip the excess net from the back of the lace close to the freehand zigzag stitch.

12 Dye the shawl an antique bronze color (test color first) using the potassium permanganate method in *Victorian Pansies* (refer to Techniques Directory on page 100 of this book). Make a slightly darker solution and use a paint brush to darken both sides of the edging lace and outside edges of the embroidery on the center and corners of the wrap. Rinse the wrap in cold water after three minutes. Remove excess water by placing wrap flat on a towel and rolling it. Unroll and lay it flat to dry.

13 Use the hand-sewing needle and thread to stitch a beaded tassel centered at the bottom of each edging lace design on the two short sides of the triangle. When complete press wrap from the wrong side over a towel to keep the embroidery raised.

This wrap will turn heads whenever you wear it and in between times looks fabulous draped over a mirror or lamp. Once you have mastered the lace techniques used in the Romantic Lace Wrap, try your hand at reproducing your version of the stunning skirt pictured opposite.

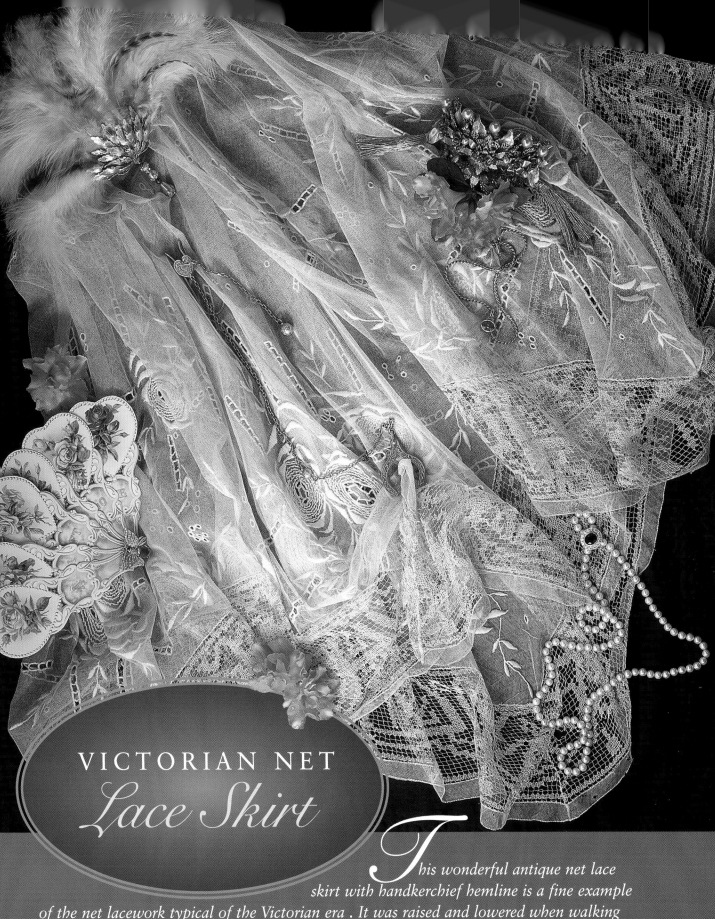

VICTORIAN NET
Lace Skirt

This wonderful antique net lace skirt with handkerchief hemline is a fine example of the net lacework typical of the Victorian era . It was raised and lowered when walking over mud or puddles with a gold Victorian skirt lifter which was attached at the waist and clipped to the hem of the dress.

31

GLAMOROUS EVENING *Bodice*

*Victorian Lace designs
such as Lace 19 can be used in many
ways and in many colors.
This richly decorated bodice reflects
the versatility of these magic lace designs
which have been stitched in black thread
down each side of the bodice then hand
beaded with iridescent black beads.
The murky green pin-striped fabric is
reminiscent of the Victorian era.*

*The front of the bodice has been pieced
then embroidered using self-adhesive
tear-away in the hoop to eliminate
the need for fabric to hoop
in the conventional way. The printed
templates and the placement stitching,
ensure perfect placement joining the lace
designs accurately following the curve of
the bodice's front shaping seams.*

*The bodice is then constructed
following the pattern instructions.
This technique can be applied to any
garment that needs a touch of lace to
add that special finish.*

*Carnival masks by Delia Clough,
see credits on page 102.*

MAGNIFICENT
Obsession Quilt

My obsession with pansies (VICTORIAN PANSIES) and the color purple
(quilt by the same name) is well known to those
who are familiar with my work. Once I had seen the pansy
tapestry fabric, I just had to have it, and the idea
for this project was born.

OBSESSION *Quilt*

*T*o promote machine embellished quilts is my mission and this was to be my first step into the traditional quilt arena.

I have designed and made many quilts, not to mention the books I have published, but never have I had a quilt entered into any quilt show— never had time I guess.

With the encouragement of my friend Narelle Grieve, together we submitted our quilts to the prestigious Houston Quilt Festival and to our delight (and my amazement) they were both accepted. And guess what. I had my quilt hung in the Houston Quilt Festival— a machine-embellished quilt!

NOTE: *The quilt blocks are embellished then joined into one piece—the quilt top. Then the batting is sandwiched between the quilt top and the backing fabric and quilted through as a whole quilt. Machine quilting a whole quilt is quite challenging because of the bulk that has to go under the sewing machine needle but once completed is quite an achievement. On the other hand if you wish to 'quilt-as-you-go' (which is much easier) then cut the batting the same size as the fabric pieces then use Helmar's quilt basting spray to fuse the batting to the back of the fabric pieces (except tapestry grid pieces, broderie perse pieces, Victorian prints and binding strips) before any work is done on them, then when complete (embroidery quilting etc.) piece the quilt, add the backing fabric and stitch-in-the-ditch through all seams to hold the quilt together. Either way the finished effect is the same. (For those who just have to have the pansy fabric, yes I do have a limited stock and you can email me for it!)*

MEASUREMENTS

Following the convention of quilting instructions, all measurements are in yards and inches.

Finished size of quilt is 70in square

- Finished size eight black fabric blocks is 14in square (1, 3, 5, 7, 9, 11, 13 and 15)
- Finished size eight tapestry blocks is 14in x 10in (2, 4, 6, 8, 10, 12, 14 and 16)
- Finished size center medallion is 28in square
- Finished size center on point square is 20in
- Finished size inside wider border is 2¼in
- Finished size inside narrow border is ⅝in
- Finished size quilt borders is 3¼in

KEY FOR QUILT

- Blocks 1, 5, 9 and 13 are tapestry grid and embroidery on black fabric.
- Blocks 2, 4, 6, 8, 10, 12, 14 and 16 are tapestry fabric.
- Blocks 3, 7, 11 and 15 are black Victorian Prints on black fabric.
- Triangles A, B, C, and D on the sides of the center square set on point are tapestry fabric.
- On point square E in center of quilt is black fabric with tapestry grid and embroidery.
- G and H are grape purple border fabrics.
- F and I are black border fabric and binding

MATERIALS

- *3yd x 60in Victorian Pansy Tapestry fabric for grid, blocks and broderie perse technique*
- *3½yd x 54in purple homespun fabric for quilt backing fabric, narrow inner border and wide quilt borders*
- *3½yd x 54in black fabric for grid and print blocks inner borders and quilt binding*
- *1 pack of Hobb's Ultra-thin Thermore Premier batting for quilting (this pack has one piece of batting suitable for a queen size quilt)*
- *2yd Vliesofix /Wonderunder double sided fusible web*
- *4 Jenny Haskins' Victorian prints— two No 1017 and two 1019*

- *Eight pieces of hand painted antique rayon lace (in VICTORIAN PANSIES, see Techniques Directory on page 100 in this book)*
- *Pfaff PC-Designer software*
- *Pfaff blank memory card*
- *Victorian Pansies CD by Jenny Haskins*
- *Victorian Butterflies CD Jenny Haskins designs from Cactus Punch*
- *Vellum (112gsm) tracing paper for templates*
- *THREADS: Madeira rayon 40 in the following colors:*

— *3 x 1000m reels olive green for grid and motif embroidery*
— *3 x 1000m reels gray mauve for grid and motif embroidery*
— *1000m reel purple thread for pansy and butterfly embroidery*
— *1000m reel black purple for pansy and butterfly embroidery*
— *1000m reel antique gold for pansy and butterfly embroidery*
— *1000m reel soft yellow for pansy and butterfly embroidery*

- *1000m reel white for pansy centers*
- *1000m reel black for butterflies and quilting*
- *1000m reel of warm brown green for embroidery on silk prints*
- *1 reel monofilament transparent thread for outline quilting and broderie perse*
- *Black and purple (to match purple backing fabric) construction thread*
- *Madeira pre-wound bobbins for machine and motif embroidery*
- *MACHINE NEEDLES: size-80 top stitch needle for embroidery, 75-universal for construction, size-60 sharp for broderie perse*
- *MACHINE FEET: open-toe embroidery foot, clear-view freehand foot, narrow edge foot and ¼-inch foot*
- *3 cans Helmar's quilt basing spray*
- *Self-adhesive tear-away stabilizer for hoop embroidery*
- *Photocopy paper used as stabilizer for built-in stitching*
- *Chalk marking pencil (make sure it comes out easily)*
- *Olfa mat, quilting rule and rotary cutter*
- *Small sharp pair of scissors—I prefer the Fiska's soft grip*
- *Quilting pins*
- *General sewing requirements*

PREPARATION

CUTTING

NB: *If you have chosen the 'quilt-as-you-go' technique remember you will need to cut the batting to suit the fabric and use the Helmar's Quilt basting spray to attach the batting to the fabric.*

1 Use the rotary cutter, Olfa mat and quilting ruler to cut the following.

FROM THE BLACK FABRIC CUT:

—eight, 16in squares for corner blocks and print blocks

—one, 22in square for the center medallion to be set on point

—four, 2¾in strips the width of the fabric for the wide inner border

—4in strips the length of the fabric for the binding

FROM THE DARK PURPLE HOMESPUN CUT:

—4¼in strips the length of the fabric for outer borders

—1¼in strips the width of the fabric for narrow inner border

—remaining fabric will be used as quilt backing

FROM VLIESOFIX/WONDERUNDER CUT:

—12in x 60in wide strip to be ironed to the back of matching strip of pansy fabric

FROM THE PANSY TAPESTRY FABRIC CUT:

—12in strip the width of the fabric then use a hot steam iron to iron the 12in wide strip of Vliesofix/Wonderunder to the back of this fabric strip

—from the width of the above 12in piece of backed fabric cut seventeen ¾in strips for lattice

NOTE: *As this floral fabric is a repeat design, you may choose to work around the pansies you wish to use for broderie perse before you cut out the following:*

—two, 14½in squares to be cut on the diagonal into four triangles for the corners of the center square set on point

—eight, 10½in x 14½in rectangles to go between the embroidered blocks

—the remaining fabric is used for the broderie perse and has Vliesofix/Wonderunder ironed to the back of where the floral designs will be cut out

2 On four of the 16in black fabric squares use the quilting ruler and the chalk marking pencil to rule a diagonal line from opposite corners that passes through the center of each block.

3 On either side of this line measure out 3½in and draw two lines parallel to the diagonal line. Continue ruling lines to the outside edge of the blocks.

4 Repeat steps 2 and 3 in the opposite direction to create an equally spaced grid. Repeat the grid lines on the large center square to be set on point.

5 Use the above lines as the center guideline to iron the ¾in tapestry fabric strips to the marked blocks, first in one direction and then in the opposite direction.

TIP: *As the tapestry fabric is thick, it is advisable to use a hot iron with plenty of steam—the ideal iron is a Pfaff industrial strength iron as this gives maximum steam.*

6 Iron the tapestry fabric strips to four corner squares and the center block to be set on point.

7 Trim the Victorian prints to measure 7½in x 11in then apply the quilt basting spray to the back of each print then center these on the remaining four black fabric squares.

TIP: *Use the quilt basting spray in a well-ventilated area—preferably outside. For small areas use a cardboard box that will contain the spray. For larger areas such as the back of a quilt, have a large cleared surface, such as the floor of your garage, with windows and doors open. Cover the area with either paper or sheeting that can be washed, making sure it exceeds the size of the quilt by at least one foot on all sides. Lay the batting on the covered floor, center the quilt top over the batting then roll the quilt top right back to one edge. Sparingly apply the basting spray across the batting for an area of one foot adjacent to the rolled-up top, let dry for around a minute, then unroll quilt top over the sprayed batting, pressing the fabric to the batting and making sure there are no puckers. Continue in this way until the whole quilt top is un-rolled and basted to the batting, then apply the backing in the same way. Be careful not to let the spray go on the right side of the fabric of either the quilt top or backing. Should the fabric move, a hot steam iron will reactivate the basting spray to secure fabrics in place until quilting is completed.*

8 The floral motifs to be used as brodeie perse should be chosen and cut out carefully around the outside edge of the pansies, making sure no background fabric is visible. Remember you can cut out individual flowers, leaves and buds to create your own design. You will need approximately 20 pansies and suitable leaves, either attached or cut out singly.

EMBROIDERY

9 Use Madeira rayon 40 thread, a size-80 top stitch needle and Madeira pre-wound bobbins for all embroidery.

10 Built-in embroidery stitches require an open-toe foot and photocopy paper as stabilizer at the back of the fabric. Remove photocopy paper after each row of stitching.

11 Hoop embroidery requires the self-adhesive tear-away stabilizer in the hoop to ensure ease of placement.

BLOCKS 3 AND 11 CENTER BLOCKS
TOP AND BOTTOM OF QUILT

12 Using the Pfaff PC-Designer software, blank card and the Jenny Haskins' Victorian Pansies CD and the Victorian Butterflies CD by Cactus Punch to transfer the following designs to the bank card:
—panspray
—butterfly 4
—butterfly 3

13 Use the Vellum (112gsm) tracing paper to print out the above designs remembering to use the 1:1 ratio when printing. Refer to page 12 for the use of templates when working with embroidery motifs.

BLOCKS 1, AND 9 CORNER BLOCKS

🍂 On either side of each tapestry strip use the olive green thread to embroider:

—stitch No 60 length 10, width 6.0 and density 0.25
—stitch No 156 length 12, width 6.0 on either side of the above rows of stitching.

🍂 Use the tracing paper templates and the photo on page 39 as a guide to colors used and positioning to stitch the following embroidery motifs in place over the embroidered tapestry grid:

—four, panspray

BLOCKS 5 AND 13 CORNER BLOCKS

🍂 On either side of each tapestry strip use the gray mauve thread to embroider:

—stitch No 60 length 10, width 6.0 and density 0.25
—stitch No 165 length and width 4.0, density 0.25 on either side of the above rows of stitching

🍂 Use the vellum (112gsm) tracing paper templates and the photo on page 39 as a guide to colors used and positioning to stitch the following embroidery motifs in place over the embroidered tapestry grid:

—four, panspray

BLOCKS 3 AND 11 CENTER BLOCKS
TOP AND BOTTOM OF QUILT

🍂 Use the photo as guide to colors used to sew the following:

—stitch No 01, length 3.0 across the grid in the center of the pansy print
—stitch No 165, width and length 6.0 density 0.25, single pattern button engaged to stitch over the intersecting lines of the grid
—stitch No 00, straight stitch, clear-view freehand foot and black thread to freehand long-stitch the pansy 'beard and whiskers' on all the pansies on the print.

🍂 **FREEHAND LONG STITCH.** Lower the feed dogs, use the clear-view freehand foot. Position the needle on one end of the line that is to be covered, bring foot into the freehand position then use a small tie off stitch to secure the thread. The foot is then dragged the length of the line ('pansy 'whisker'), tie off with a stitch, then drag the stitch back over the previous long stitch and again tie off over the first tie-off stitch. Take a small stitch to the left or right,

(depending on the direction you wish to move in) tie off, drag, tie off, and repeat the above until all the lines ('pansy beard and whiskers') are covered with these long stitches accenting the area round the pansy face. The trick is to follow the direction of the lines on the pansy to achieve a three dimensional effect.

🍂 Use the above thread, needle and foot to stipple stitch the plain background of the print to secure it to the fabric block.

—stitch No 16 width 2.0, density 0.6 embroidered around the outside edge of the pansy print to cover the raw fabric edges.

—stitch No 83, width and length normal embroidered on the outside edge of the above stitch

❧ Iron Vliesofix/Wonderunder to the back of the hand painted lace (covered in *Victorian Pansies*, refer to Techniques Directory on page 100 of this book). Use the photo as a guide to positioning the lace then iron in place.

NOTE: *You may need to cut the lace into suitable segments to shape it nicely around the corners.*

❧ Use the monofilament thread, clear-view freehand foot and a straight stitch to freehand sew the lace in place following the lace outline. Remember to secure any cut ends to prevent unraveling.

BLOCK 7 AND 15 CENTERED BLOCKS ON EITHER SIDE OF THE QUILT

❧ Use the photo as guide to colors used to sew the following:

—stitch No 01 length 3.0 across the grid in the center of the heart

—stitch No 60 length 10 width 6.0 density 0.25 around the edge of the heart, with the straight edge of the design aligned with the edge of the heart and the scallops facing to the center of the heart

❧ Repeat the edge stitching, the stipple stitch, the lace corners and the freehand long stitching in the center of the pansies in the same manner as for blocks 3 and 11.

CENTER MEDALLION CENTER BLOCK SET ON POINT (DIAMOND)

❧ Embroider the tapestry strips using the same thread and stitches as for blocks 1 and 9.

❧ Use the Vellum (112gsm) tracing paper templates and the photo as a guide to colors used and positioning to stitch the following embroidery motifs in place over the embroidered tapestry grid:

—five, panspray in the shape of an 'S'

—two, butterfly 4, using black thread as the background color

—one, butterfly 3, using black thread as the background color

❧ Remove all excess stabilizer from the back of the block and chalk pencil marks from the front of the block, then press from the wrong side over a towel.

ATTACHING THE TAPESTRY TRIANGLES

❧ Square the block to 20½in.

❧ Use construction thread in needle and bobbin and the ¼-inch foot to sew the tapestry triangles to each side of the embroidered center diamond, ensuring that they overlap ¼in in the center of the block.

❧ Trim the center medallion to 20½in square.

ATTACHING THE BORDERS TO THE CENTER MEDALLION

❧ Use construction thread in the needle and bobbin and the ¼-inch foot to sew the 1¼in purple fabric strips to one side of the 2¾in black fabric strips to be used as borders for the center medallion.

❧ Attach one of these strips, black fabric edge to edge of center medallion, to the top and bottom, then to either side of the center medallion.

❧ Press all seams and put to one side.

JOINING THE BLOCKS

Use the photo on page 37 as a guide to the direction and position of each block, pinning before sewing together.

Remove all excess stabilizer from the back of the embroidered blocks and chalk pencil marks from the front of the blocks, then press from the wrong side over a towel.

Maintain the center of the blocks and trim to 14½in square.

TOP AND BOTTOM ROW OF BLOCKS

❧ Attach tapestry rectangle (blocks No. 2 and No. 4) to either side of block No. 3 (top row).

❧ Attach a tapestry rectangle (blocks No. 12 and 10) to either side of block No. 11 so the print faces to the lower edge of the row and ensuring the tapestry blocks are all facing the same direction.

❧ Attach these strips to the top and bottom of the center medallion respectively.

SIDE ROWS OF BLOCKS

❧ Attach block No. 1, No. 16, No. 15, No. 14 and No. 13 together for the left side of the quilt making sure the print faces to the outside of the row.

❧ Attach block No. 5, No. 6, No. 7 No. 8 and No. 9 together for the right side of the quilt making sure the print faces to the outside of the row.

❧ Attach these two rows to the left and right sides of the quilt respectively.

QUILT BORDERS

❧ Attach the purple 4¼in border strips to the top and bottom and then the sides of the quilt.

BRODERIE PERSE

Use the photos as a guide to position and direction of the cut out floral fabric pieces that are to be used for broderie perse. Pin in place then use a hot steam iron to press the pieces in place.

When applying these pieces remember to place them over the whole tapestry fabric sections so they appear to be part of these pieces and extend into the plain fabric areas.

Use monofilament thread, size-60 needle, clear-view freehand foot, a pre-wound bobbin and a small zigzag stitch for broderie perse technique explained in *Victorian Roses* (see Techniques Directory, page 100 of this book).

QUILTING

Refer to the Quilt Basting Technique in step 7 to apply the quilt basting spray to sandwich the batting between the quilt top and backing, making sure the batting and backing extend at least 1in on all sides of the quilt.

TIP: *When quilting a whole quilt it is advisable to clear a well lit large area with three to four feet of support around your machine. It is preferable to have the bed of the machine level with these supports—a machine quilting cabinet is well worth the investment. Roll the quilt up into a manageable size, on all four sides of the center, these can be held in place with bicycle clips. Quilting a whole quilt is always done from the center out.*

Wind 20 machine bobbins with construction thread to match the color of the backing fabric.

Use the narrow edge foot, size-75 universal needle and monofilament thread and a straight stitch to quilt the following:

—either side of the embroidered tapestry strips close to the straight side of the embroidered scallops

—stitch-in-the-ditch in all seams

Use the clear-view freehand foot, size-75 universal needle, a straight stitch and monofilament thread to quilt the following:

—outline quilt all the machine embroidered motifs

—outline quilt all the pansies on the tapestry fabric

—outline quilt around all the broderie perse floral motifs

Use the clear-view freehand foot, size-75 universal needle, a straight stitch and black thread to stipple-quilt the following:

—the black border fabric around the center medallion

—the black fabric surrounding the four blocks with the Victorian prints

Use the open-toe foot, size-75 universal needle, purple thread and a straight stitch to quilt around the purple fabric borders of the quilt with two equally spaced rows of stitching (1in apart starting from the border seam.)

FINISHING THE QUILT

Trim and square the quilt to a size of 70in square.

Use the 4in black fabric binding strips to bind the edge of the quilt using a ½in seam allowance using your preferred method of binding. Quilt binding is covered in *Victorian Roses*, refer to Techniques Directory on page 100 of this book.

CENTER MEDALLION
CENTER BLOCK SET ON POINT (DIAMOND)

43

Wendy Fenwick is an award winning doll maker who is Victorian at heart so when she saw the Victorian Lace CD she just had to use the embroidery for this exquisitely dressed doll.

The doll, also made by Wendy using an antique German mold, can be obtained in kit form (see page 102).

Instructions are given here for the dress, bonnet, bag and jacket. Remaining instructions for the petticoat and pantaloons are on the CD accompanying this book.

DOLL SIZE 41CM (16IN) HEIGHT

MATERIALS

- 40cm (16in) crinkled shot viscose printed fabric for dolls dress
- 50cm (20in) satin for jacket, hat and bag
- 50cm (20in) voile, net or any other lightweight fabric
- 40cm (16in) lining fabric for the jacket
- 15cm (6in) contrast fabric for bonnet lining
- 15cm (6in) heavyweight interfacing for bonnet
- 25cm (10in) woven interfacing for pleating
- 1.4m x 1.5cm (54in x ¾in) scalloped edging lace, dyed to match the jacket fabric (darker than the dress)
- 50cm x 4cm (20in x 1½in) wire-edged ribbon for bonnet
- 20cm x 1cm (8in x ⅜in) antique gold braid for bonnet
- 1m x 1cm (1yd x ⅜in) ribbon for bonnet and hair
- 15cm (6in) beaded lace trim to match edging lace for inside bonnet brim
- 10cm x 5cm (4in x 2in) beaded fringe for dress and bag to match color of jacket
- 2m (2⅛yd) silk ribbon flower tape for the bottom of the petticoat, neck and bottom of pantaloons
- 6mm (¼in) wide elastic to fit waist of doll
- 1 packet small beads to match the above color to bead the embroidered motifs

- 1 packet of antique seed beads to bead the side of the purse
- Beading needle and thread
- 4 x 6mm (¼in) diameter buttons for the back of the dress
- 8 clear snaps for back of dress and petticoat
- Fine Easy Pleater
- Spray starch
- Rajah pressing-cloth
- Pfaff PC-Designer software
- Pfaff blank memory card
- Pfaff Victorian Lace CD by Jenny Haskins
- Self-adhesive tear-away stabilizer for hoop embroidery
- Romeo water-soluble stabilizer for stand-alone embroidery for front of dress
- MACHINE FEET: ¼-inch foot, normal sewing foot
- MACHINE NEEDLES: size-80 embroidery needle and size–75 universal needle
- THREADS: Madeira rayon 40 to match jacket color and gold metallic thread, cotton construction thread
- Madeira pre-wound bobbins for embroidery
- Hand sewing needle
- Tracing paper and lead pencil
- Vellum (112gsm) tracing paper for printing out embroidery templates
- Chalk pencil
- General sewing requirements

PREPARATION

Use the tracing paper and lead pencil to trace the pattern pieces from the pattern sheet then cut them out.

CONSTRUCTION

NOTE: *All pattern pieces have a 6mm (¼in) seam allowance and require the ¼-inch foot, normal sewing foot, construction thread and the 75-universal needle when assembled.*

DRESS

1 Use the small size Easy Pleater to pleat a 25cm (10in) strip across the width of the dress fabric to make a 25cm (10in) pleated square, placing the wrong side of the fabric uppermost in the pleater. While the fabric is still in the pleater, steam press the pleats using spray starch and a Rajah pressing cloth. Cut a piece of woven interfacing the same size as the pleated fabric. Heat bond the interfacing to the wrong side of the pleats, allow to cool then remove by rolling the pleater off fabric.

2 Pin pieces No. 5, No. 6 and No. 8 on the dress fabric and cut out. Cut out the 26cm (10¼in) fabric strip the width of the fabric for the skirt. Cut out the center front skirt panel (pattern piece No. 7a) from the pleated fabric square.

3 Stitch shoulder seams of the bodice for both the dress and the lining (backs to front bodice pieces).

4 Press seams flat. Join the dress bodice and lining, right sides together and stitching from wrong side of the fabric, around the neck and center back. Trim and clip seams then turn to the right side.

5 Stitch the scalloped edging lace around the right side of the neck edge turning the ends to the underside of the bodice at the center back openings.

6 Gather up the sleeves following the gathering line, to fit the armhole on the bodice. Pin in place, right sides together, matching center top of sleeve with the shoulder seam and stitch in place from the wrong side of the fabric.

7 To puff up the sleeves, cut out a 12.5cm (5in) diameter circle of fabric, fold in half then run a gathering stitch along the cut edges of the resulting double-fabric half circle. Pull up the gathers to make a straight line with the folded edge erect. Center the gathered edge over the seam line of the head of the sleeve then stitch in place over the seam line. Repeat for second sleeve and cut away excess fabric from around the armholes then machine-neaten.

8 Turn a hem under on the bottom of each sleeve then attach the dyed scalloped lace to the right side of hem so the lace sits over the edge of the hem.

9 With right sides of fabric together and stitching from the wrong side, join the underarm sleeve seams following through to the side seams of the bodice to complete the bodice.

10 Fold the skirt fabric strip in half (center back) then cut down 7.5cm (3in) from the top edge of the strip to sew a center placket in the back of the skirt using your preferred method.

11 With right sides of fabric together with raw edges aligned join either side edge of the skirt strip to either side of the center pleated skirt panel.

12 On the right side, sew the edging lace over the above seams on either side of the pleated panel so the scallops face out and are matched on either side (see photo). Machine neaten the bottom edge of the skirt and turn up a 1.5cm (½in) hem then use the hand

sewing needle and thread to hem the skirt.

13 Gather up the skirt top to fit the bottom edge of the bodice, pin in place (right sides together) matching the center front panel to the front of the bodice and the center back placket to back opening in the bodice. Stitch in place from the wrong side of the fabric.

14 Hand sew the snaps down the center back opening of the bodice, then sew the small buttons down the center back matching the snaps.

BONNET, BAG & *Jacket*

15 Pin the pattern pieces for the jacket, bonnet and bag (Nos. 9 to 13) to the satin fabric, and then cut out. From the lining fabric cut out the lining for the jacket and the purse.

16 From contrasting lining fabric and heavyweight interfacing cut out lining for bonnet (Nos. 10 to 12.)

17 Measure up 8cm (3¼in) from the bottom hem edge of the jacket and draw an embroidery line here in chalk pencil parrallel to the edge. Mark center vertical jacket back. Draw another line midway between the embroidery line and the hem edge for lace.

EMBROIDERY

Use the Pfaff Victorian Lace CD, PC-Designer software and Lace19c to bring this design on screen then use the software to delete connecting bars at the beginning of the design. Transfer this design to a blank card (for stitching) and print on tracing paper (for a template).

JACKET
---

18 Use the placement template to position seven Lace19c evenly spaced and centered on the first drawn line with the first design centered on the center back line—three designs are evenly spaced on either side of this center design.

19 Use the self-adhesive tear-away in the hoop, gold metallic thread and dark thread to match the jacket fabric, size-80 embroidery needle and Madeira pre-wound bobbins to embroider the seven two-tone Lace19c designs around the bottom of the jacket.

20 Use the normal sewing foot, matching thread to lace and fabric and the size 75-universal needle to sew the dyed scalloped lace around the bottom of the jacket centered over the lace-placement line.

21 Use the beading needle and thread to stitch five beads around the top section of each embroidered motif.

22 Pin the jacket lining to the jacket, right sides together, and stitch from the wrong side around the outside edge of the jacket, using the ¼in foot, leaving a 15cm (6in) turning opening in the center back on the hemline. Trim seams and clip curves then turn to the right side and press, folding the turning opening and around the armholes to the inside of the jacket. Use a hand sewing needle and matching thread to slipstitch around the armholes and to close the opening.

BONNET

23 Stitch the interfacing to the wrong side of the satin fabric of the three bonnet pieces. Use a straight stitch and sew close to the edge of the fabric.

24 With right sides of fabric together and stitching from the wrong side, attach the back edge of the bonnet crown to the curved edge of the bonnet back, easing it to fit. Then attach the bonnet brim to the front edge of the bonnet crown. Trim seams and clip all edges.

25 Using the lining pieces, attach the bonnet crown to **THE BONNET BACK ONLY** in the same manner.

26 With right sides together and stitching from the wrong sides, attach the crown lining and back lining assembly to the matching pieces of the bonnet along the short sides and neck edge of the bonnet crown. Trim all seams and clip curves then turn to the right side, and push the lining inside the bonnet.

27 In the same way attach the lining to the brim of the bonnet, stitching around the outside curve of the brim only, then turn to the right side and press.

28 Turn under a hem on the inside curve of the brim lining and pin over the crown lining edge. Use the hand sewing needle and a slip stitch to sew in place.

29 Remove the wire from one side of the wire-edged ribbon, turn under the cut ends then gather up the ribbon to fit the front edge of the crown. Pin gathered ribbon to the wrong side of the narrow gold braid (right side of gathered ribbon to wrong side of braid) then pin in place at the brim/crown seam from the right side of the braid.

30 Use a hand sewing needle and thread to stitch the braid and ribbon around the right side of the crown of the bonnet so gold braid sits flat against the crown and the ribbon extends over the brim. Cut two 25cm (10in) lengths of the narrow ribbon and catch one on either side of the bonnet under the turned-under edge of the wired ribbon and stitch in place.

BAG

31 Use the chalk marking pencil to trace around the bag pattern piece No 13 three times with a 5cm (2in) gap between each one, then embroider Lace19c with gold metallic thread only in the center of each drawn pattern piece as was done on the bottom of the jacket.

32 Retrace the pattern pieces then cut them out. Cut out bag lining using the pattern pieces and lining fabric.

33 With right sides together but leaving a small opening at the base of the bag, join the side seams of three embroidered bag sections. Trim all seams and clip curves then turn to the right side and poke the fabric to the inside of the bag at the bottom opening. Cut a piece of beaded fringe so the piece has four hanging beads, roll up the ribbon edge into a small ball and push it up inside the bag through the lower opening. Use the hand-sewing needle to stitch hanging beads in place and close the opening.

34 Make a twisted cord 12cm (5in) long knotted at both ends (see Techniques Directory on page 100).

35 Stitch the lining as for bag but do not leave an opening at the bottom. Place the lining inside the bag, wrong side of lining to wrong side of bag and raw edges matching, turn a hem to the inside at the top and pin. Position a knotted end of the twisted cord equally spaced on either side of the bag top opening, so the knot sits inside the purse between the lining and the bag. Slipstitch around the top edge of the bag holding the bag, the lining and the twisted cord in place. Stitch the small beads down the outside edge of each seam using the beading needle and thread.

FINISHING THE DRESS

36 Embroider Lace19c on a piece of dress fabric placed in the hoop over Romeo in thread colors that

match those on the jacket. Remove the embroidery from the hoop, cut excess stabilizer from the back of the fabric then wash the stabilizer from the embroidery, dry then press before cutting the design out around the outside edge of the embroidery.

37 Sew the small beads on the embroidered motif using the photo as a guide, using the beading needle and thread. Then use the hand sewing needle and construction thread to sew the beaded motif to the center front of the dress bodice above the gathered skirt. Catch three beaded drops from the beaded fringe, centered under the beaded motif, so they fall over the pleated center front panel.

*T*his shawl is created using the designs on the CD accompanying this book and looks equally appealing stitched out on cream silk.

The original was freehand embroidered using a hoop so each of the four segments that make up the center design (as opposed to the borders) are slightly different.

The CD, Antique Victorian Piano Shawl by Jenny Haskins, has over 60 individual designs on it which, when stitched out on fabric and arranged in sequence to join together, form an embroidered 71cm (28in) square. This is then trimmed with a bead-edged long fringe or hanging lace and is a replica of the original.

Follow the written instructions carefully, refer to the placement pattern on the pattern sheet and the layout diagram and numbering on the CD and this will be a highly rewarding embroidery project. The embroidery designs are numbered according to their placement and each center design is slightly different. Once the technique is mastered this shawl is easy to make, but for those who want something a little less complex then the same center design can be embroidered in each quarter.

The embroidery colors used in Victorian piano shawls were usually very strong primary and secondary colors, but I have chosen to tone them down a little by using similar colored threads that are slightly grayed and therefore softer and more muted.

MATERIALS

- 87.5cm (34½in) square black fabric—for your first attempt I recommend a black cotton fabric
- 4m x 25cm (4½yd x 10in) black fringe
- 4m (4½yd) black beading to be hand sewn to the head of the fringe
- Pfaff PC-Designer software
- Pfaff Creative memory card
- CD accompanying this book, Jenny Haskins Victorian Piano Shawl
- Self-adhesive tear-away stabilizer
- MACHINE FEET: open-toe foot
- MACHINE NEEDLES: size-80 embroidery needle
- THREADS: Madeira rayon 40 embroidery thread in three shades of pink/red, olive green, gray mauve, purple, soft blue, soft lemon yellow, yellow ochre and soft apricot
- Black construction thread
- Madeira pre-wound bobbins
- Clover chalk marking pencil (pink/blue) which can be ironed, washes out of black fabric easily
- Vellum (112 gsm) tracing paper to print out placement templates
- Tracing paper to trace placement pattern from the pattern sheet
- Lead pencil
- Long quilting ruler
- General sewing requirements

PREPARATION

NOTE: *Print out the shawl layout diagram and layout overview from the CD that comes with this book and trace the placement diagram from the pattern sheet for Corner4 (top right corner).*

1 Divide the 87.5cm (34½in) fabric square in half, quarters and eighths on the vertical, horizontal and then both diagonals by folding. Use the chalk pencil and the ruler to mark these lines; the fabric is now divided into eight equal parts.

2 Measure 41cm (16⅛in) from the center on horizontal and vertical lines. At these points draw lines with the ruler and chalk pencil parallel to the sides of the fabric square to make four 41cm (16⅛in) squares. These lines also form an 82cm (32¼in) square centered on the black fabric, the perimeter of which is the cutting line for the shawl—do NOT cut.

3 Measure 5cm (2in) in from the cutting line on four sides and mark then rule lines to connect the marks to make another square 5cm (2in) inside the first drawn square (cutting line).

PIANO

Shawl

4 Draw another square 2.5cm (1in) inside the square drawn in step 3, measuring and marking accurately. This is the border (side) embroidery placement line.

5 Divide each of the four squares drawn in step 4 into four equal triangles by ruling two lines on the diagonal that connect opposite corners and intersect in the middle of each square. These are the diagonal lines.

WORKING ON CORNER4 (TOP RIGHT HAND CORNER)

(See placement pattern from pattern sheet.)

6 On the 5cm (2in) marked line drawn in step 3 measure 12cm (4¾in) from the corner on both sides and mark. Connect these two marks. The intersection of this line and the diagonal line is the center position of the corner design.

7 Plot a line parallel to and 1.5cm (½in) above each diagonal line and where they intersect is the center placement point (x) of the large embroidered flower (Center21) from which all other embroidery placements are determined.

8 Use the Pfaff PC-Designer software, the Victorian Piano Shawl CD and the Vellum (112gsm) tracing paper to print out all the designs on the CD, or if you choose to repeat the same center, the designs that are designated to that quarter only (say Center12–21) and the border embroideries—Corner1 to Corner4 and sides 1_1, 1_2, 1_3, 1_4 and 1_5 through to to 4_1, 4_2, 4_3 and so on. These are your placement templates.

9 Refer to page 12 for the markings and the use of templates.

NOTE: *The placement lines on the pattern sheet are*

drawn on the DIAGONAL *(not the vertical and horizontal) for ease as each quarter segment (called 'Centers') of the overall design is on the diagonal. You may choose to use vertical and horizontal lines that pass through the center of the printed-out design as well to correspond with the vertical and horizontal markings on the hoop, but use the diagonal lines to match over the pattern sheet.*

10 Carefully cut out the large center flower design (Center21) then using the placement lines on the template and the fabric, position the template over the fabric matching the lines exactly, and draw the flower shape with the chalk pencil.

EMBROIDERY

All embroidery requires self-adhesive tear-away stabilizer in the hoop, size-80 embroidery needle, rayon-40 embroidery thread and Madeira pre-wound bobbins.

NOTE: *Transfer the designs from the CD to the Pfaff memory card on a need-to-use basis using the software and the Creative Card Station for convenience. For example download all the corners (Corner1 through Corner4) and stitch them out, then delete them and working in a clockwise direction download and stitch border side 1_1, 1_2 etc. and then delete and so on for all side borders of the shawl.*

11 Use the corner/side border placement lines on the fabric, the placement template and the photo (as a guide to choose colors that best match those in the photo) to embroider the four corner border designs (Corner1 through Corner4).

12 Use the border placement line on the fabric and the templates to position the side border designs in number sequence. Use the photo as a guide to colors used. Embroider Side1 (1_1 to 1_5) starting to the left of Corner1, moving clockwise in number sequence. Refer to layout diagram on CD to embroider all side borders.

13 Use the traced placement diagram from the pattern sheet and the templates to draw the placement guidelines on the black fabric with a chalk pencil on the top right hand corner of the shawl. Position then embroider the designs from the lowest (Center12) finishing with the highest (Center21) to complete one quarter of the center. The last design to be embroidered is the large feature flower, Center21. Use the photo as a guide to colors or select your own.

14 Repeat the above for the remaining 3 quarters of the center (all 4 quarters will be the same) or employ the same technique but follow the number sequences for the embroidery designs indicated on the layout diagram on the CD to replicate the original hand-embroidered antique piano shawl.

15 Remove excess stabilizer from the back of the fabric, clip all threads and wash out chalk marking lines—dry flat then press with right side over a towel to keep the embroidery raised.

16 Turn a narrow hem to the right side of the fabric on all sides of the shawl, then use black construction thread and a straight stitch to hem the shawl, sewing from the right side of the fabric.

17 Position the fringe on the right side of the fabric with the fringe header sitting over the hem, pleating the corners, and stitch in place around the edge of the shawl.

18 Use the hand-sewing needle and thread to sew the black beads over the fringe header to complete the shawl.

19 Should you choose to use silk as was the case with the cream shawl (pictured opposite), then use a liquid fabric stabilizer such as Helmar's Sew Stable, ⅔ stabilizer to ⅓ water. Allow drying then press with a hot steam iron true to grain. Use a fabric-marking pen to draw placement lines then embroider as for the above using Romeo sprayed with an adhesive such as a basting spray and the stick and sew technique (see page 14) to place the fabric over the Romeo. Repeat steps 16–19 to complete the shawl.

*T*his project also incorporates built-in stitches and broderie perse; a method of applying printed fabric motifs such as flowers, leaves and butterflies which have been cut out from printed fabric and applied with almost invisible stitches to a background fabric (see page 46 of VICTORIAN ROSES book for the history of broderie perse and page 97 of the same publication for the machine-stitched version of this technique). The whole concept could also be adapted to the center of a quilt or a feature on the back of a vest or jacket. So the project will blend with your own décor, choose fabric borders from your own home furnishing fabrics.

FINISHED SIZE OF QUILT 24½ INCH SQUARE.

Following the convention of quilting instructions, all measurements are in inches.

MATERIALS

- Victorian Rose print (No. 1051) by Jenny Haskins centered in a 19in fabric square of either muslin or delustered satin for the center (see note, right)
- Backing fabric muslin 25in square
- Border fabric muslin 2 x (3in x 25in) and 2 x (3in x 27in) strips
- Rose fabric 2 x (4in x 56in) strips for borders
- Rose fabric pieces with rose designs suitable for broderie perse
- Wonderunder/Vliesofix to fix the above

- Fusible batting 24in square
- *THREADS:* Madeira rayon 40 embroidery: choose threads that best match the rose border fabric— two shades of pink for roses and built-in stitch embroidery, yellow for the center of roses, two shades of green for leaves, lace embroidery, freehand leaves and crosshatch lines, metallic gold No 3 for stipple-quilting
- Monofilament thread for broderie perse
- Madeira pre-wound bobbins
- Construction thread
- Embroidery design CDs: Jenny Haskins Pfaff Victorian Lace and Victorian Roses
- Pfaff PC-Designer software and blank card
- Pfaff large hoop
- *MACHINE FEET:* open-toe foot, ¼in foot, clear-view freehand foot
- *MACHINE NEEDLES:* Size-80 top embroidery needle and size-60 sharp needle
- Glitter glue for simulated beads
- Vellum (112gsm) tracing paper for printing embroidery templates
- Teflon pressing mat
- Self-adhesive tear-away for hoop embroidery
- Helmar's quilt basting spray
- General sewing requirements

NOTE: *The Victorian Rose print used for this project was printed in the center of a 19in square of delustered satin which can be bought as a special order. However, a standard print can be fixed to the center of a right-sized square of fabric of your choice. Trim print to the edge of the motif or cut the fabric beyond the print to the measurements of the rectangle (see step 2) then attach to the satin square with Wonderunder/Vliesofix or machine stitching, centers matching and wrong side of print to right side of fabric square. This is now called the 'rose print' in the instructions. The raw edges of the print can be completely disguised with built-in stitch embroidery around the oval or embroidered lace motifs around the rectangle.*

PREPARATION

1 Cut all fabric pieces to the measurements in the materials list. Iron Wonderunder/Vliesofix to the back of the roses and leaves to be used for broderie perse and cut them out carefully around the outside edge of the designs.

ROMANTIC ROSE
Table Quilt

❧⸳❧⸳❧

This elaborately embellished table quilt or wall hanging features embroidery designs from my Victorian Roses and Victorian Lace CDs combined with freehand embroidery and quilting.

2 Fold the rose print in half vertically then horizontally to find its center. Use the fabric marking pen and ruler to draw an 11½in x 9½in rectangle to surround the rose print, ensuring that its sides are equidistant from the print border. Mark the center of each side of the rectangle with an intersecting line using the fabric-marking pen, which will be the center placement position for Lace20a and b.

3 Use the Pfaff software and blank card to transfer the following designs.

PLEASE NOTE: *If all the designs do not fit on the blank card at the one time, delete a design when you have stitched it out in order to fit the new design on to the card.*

FROM VICTORIAN LACE:
—lace20a and 20b
—lace20c

FROM VICTORIAN ROSES:
—sopenros
—sleaf1
—sleaf2

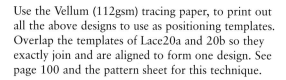

Use the Vellum (112gsm) tracing paper, to print out all the above designs to use as positioning templates. Overlap the templates of Lace20a and 20b so they exactly join and are aligned to form one design. See page 100 and the pattern sheet for this technique.

EMBROIDERY MOTIFS

Use the photo and the rose print as a guide to colors used and marked rectangles and Vellum (112gsm) tracing paper templates for positioning and direction of embroidery. For all embroidery use a size-80 embroidery needle, rayon 40 embroidery thread and Madeira pre-wound bobbins in the bobbin.

TIP: *Dense embroidery such as these motifs should be pressed using a Teflon mat that sits either over the right side or under the right side of the embroidery that is pressed either from the front or back with a hot steam iron. This ensures that the fabric is stretched between embroidering the motifs and remains flat and smooth at all times and that the print is not damaged.*

4 Use the self-adhesive tear-away technique (refer to Techniques Directory page 100) in the normal/120 hoop to embroider the leaves first over the leaves on the rose print then the center rose, then the roses on either side overlapping the center rose. The roses slightly overlap the leaves and each other giving a three dimensional effect.

5 Use the self-adhesive tear-away technique in the large hoop to embroider Lace 20a and 20b centered over each side of the rectangle using the intersecting lines on either side of the rectangle as the center of the long design. See page 100 in this book for use of the large hoop.

Repeat for the remaining three sides of the rectangle.

Use the Vellum (112gsm) tracing paper template of Lace20c to mark the corner placement positions on the drawn rectangle. Embroider this design centered over each corner, so as to join the long lace designs, using normal/120 hoop and self-adhesive tear-away.

Press the embroidered center fabric, then straighten and square it.

CONSTRUCTION

6 Use the ¼-inch foot, construction thread and a straight stitch to join the border fabric to the outside edge of the embroidered center fabric using mitered corners (refer to Techniques Directory page 100). You may choose to use your open-toe foot, green embroidery thread, straight stitch and needle positions to top stitch around the edges and the mitered corners to give a finish to the border fabric.

7 Use the photo as a guide to positioning cut-out roses and leaves in opposite corners making sure the leaves sit under the flowers, then iron to fix.

8 Iron the fusible batting to the back of the block then use the basting spray to apply the backing fabric to the back of the batting (see page 39) and iron in place from right side of the backing fabric (make sure Teflon pressing mat is under the center of the print).

BUILT-IN STITCH EMBROIDERY

For all built-in stitch embroidery use an open-toe foot, size-80 embroidery needle, rayon 40 embroidery thread, Madeira pre-wound bobbins, the 'dual feed' engaged and photocopy paper as stabilizer when recommended. Use your single pattern (tie off) for the beginning and end of each row and the photo as a guide to thread colors used.

9 On paper, draw a circle with a radius of 2¾in then cut it out and fold it in half. Use this template and the fabric-marking pen to draw half circles that are centered on each corner of the lace-covered rectangle.

10 Use the following stitches to complete the embroidery on the quilt:

—stitch No. 1 (top stitch) to stitch over the grid lines in the center of the rose print

—stitch No. 60 (satin stitch scallop) width and length 6, density 0.25 to embroider around the outside edge of the oval covering the edge of the grid stitching and the outside edge of the corner half circles (use photocopy paper at the back for stabilizer)

—stitch No. 1 (topstitch) length 1.5 along the straight edge of the satin stitch scallops embroidered above

—stitch No. 165 (small satin stitch ball) width and length 3.0, density 0.25 along the inside edge of the above stitch over the grid lines of the center oval then change to width and length 6.0, single pattern button on, to embroider over the center of each circular lace embroidery design using photocopy paper at the back for stabilizer

—stitch No. 165 (small satin stitch ball) width and length 4.0, density 0.25, twin needle button engaged to reduce the size of the stitch yet again and single pattern button on, at the top of each scallop around the central oval. Clip the connecting threads

—stitch No. 50 (scallop with open inside stitches) width and length 6.0 around the outside edge of the corner half circles and on the inside edge of border fabric on all four sides of the quilt using the normal width and length

FREEHAND EMBROIDERY/QUILTING

Use the clear-view freehand foot, feed dogs lowered, a pre-wound bobbin and size-80 embroidery needle for gold and green thread and size-60 sharp needle for monofilament thread and the photo as a guide to freehand quilt, outline embroider and stitch designs.

11 Use the gold metallic thread and small continuous meandering lines to stipple quilt the center of the quilt.

12 Use the fabric-marking pen to draw in leaves around the broderie perse roses and leaves then freehand the outlines and veins with three throws of stitching.

13 Use the monofilament thread and stitch No 2 (zig zag) width 2 to stitch down and seal all the raw fabric edges of the cut out roses and leaves (broderie perse). Change to a straight stitch to outline quilt around the outside edge of the lace, roses and leaf embroidery to quilt and define the embroidery.

COMPLETING THE QUILT

14 Press the quilt then square and straighten the edges.

15 Join the binding strips if necessary to fit the top and bottom of the quilt and the longer sides of the quilt and attach binding (refer to Techniques Directory page 100, Quilt Binding).

16 Use the glitter pen to highlight the stamens in the center of the embroidered roses and the intersections of the stitch grid in the center oval to simulate small beads. Allow to dry thoroughly before handling.

This quilt would grace any Victorian table, or by adding a casing or hangers would look equally spectacular on the wall.

VICTORIAN HIGH TEA
Tablecloth

The centre of this tablecloth is the main attraction and is isolated here as a spectacular doily.

58

HIGH TEA
Tablecloth

Techniques in this tablecloth can be adapted to almost anything. Use the center section only and cut around the edge for a beautiful doily.

Stitch it over fine net or black satin, for an entirely different effect.

NOTE: *I used a scalloped edge purchased tablecloth, measuring 79cm (31in) square with a self-trim. You may choose to do this or create your own, marking out a scalloped edge and rounded corners trimmed with your own machine-embroidered lace.*

MATERIALS

- *Linen, cotton, voile or net 89cm (35in) square— allows for scalloped edge, or a purchased 79cm (31in) square tablecloth*
- *1.5m (59in) melt-away*
- *Pfaff PC-Designer software*
- *Pfaff Creative memory card*
- *Pfaff Victorian Lace CD by Jenny Haskins*
- *MACHINE FEET: open-toe foot*
- *MACHINE NEEDLES: size-80 topstitch needle and 120-wing needle*
- *THREADS: Madeira white Tanne/Cotona 80 thread and rayon 40 embroidery thread in a contrasting color*
- *Madeira pre-wound bobbins*
- *Helmar's quilt basting spray*
- *Photocopy paper for stabilizer*
- *Vellum (112gsm) tracing paper to print out placement template*
- *Quilting ruler*
- *Heavy duty spray starch such as Crisp*
- *Small sharp scissors*
- *General sewing requirements*

PREPARATION

Press the cloth/fabric using at least three coats of spray starch. Iron in between each coat paying particular attention to the edge of the cloth which is to be embroidered with rows of built-in stitches.

1 Fold either the tablecloth or the fabric to be used for the tablecloth in half vertically, horizontally and diagonally, then fold in half again on the diagonal to divide the cloth through the center into 16ths. Press with a hot steam iron to give sharp fold lines. It is very important to do this accurately so that each line passes directly through the center of the cloth. If making your own table cloth, draw TWO shallow scallops to span each segment edge adjacent to the corners. Draw one scallop only to span each of the remaining eight segments. Each corner has two scallops (one either side of the diagonal) and there are four scallops between the corner scallops.

2 Use the fabric-marking pen and quilting ruler to mark in all lines and scallops (if making your own cloth) .

3 On the vertical, horizontal and corner diagonal lines, measure from the center out towards the edge of the tablecloth 11.5cm (4½in) then use the fabric marking pen to mark these points. Use these points to position embroidery design Lace1 from Victorian Lace by Pfaff.

4 On the angled lines that divide the cloth into 16ths, that is every alternate line not marked for placement so far, measure from the center out 19.5cm (7¾in) then use the fabric marking pen to mark these points. This is to position Lace9 from Victorian Lace by Pfaff.

5 Use the Pfaff PC-Designer software and a blank card to load Lace1, Lace9, Lace6 and the Lace20c. Remember you may not have enough memory on one card to fit all these designs at once, as they are so memory intense.

6 Print out the above designs on Vellum (112gsm) tracing paper, see page 12 for template technique.

7 Use the above technique to position the embroidery designs on their respective lines and connect the dots and mark the starting positions.

8 If you have a store-bought cloth as I have, you may need to find the center diagonal lines of the existing scalloped corners (mine were different from the true diagonal corner folds). Press a corner flat, then fold corner so first scallops match and corner is divided diagonally in two (this will be a different fold from the previously folded and diagonally drawn lines). Draw in this new line and open out flat.

Measure from corner point along the edge of tablecloth 10cm (4in) on both sides of the corner and mark. Draw a line that connects both these marks. Where these two new lines intersect is the center positioning mark for Lace6, which is embroidered in each corner of the cloth. Repeat for the other three corners.

BUILT-IN STITCH EMBROIDERY

All built-in stitch embroidery requires photocopy paper as stabilizer at the back of the fabric for satin stitches, an open-toe foot (with 'dual feet' engaged), Madeira pre-wound bobbin and Tanne/Cotona 80 in the needle.

9 The following built-in stitches are embroidered around the edge of the tablecloth following either the drawn-in or existing scallops with the first row close to the edge of the scallops

NOTE: *If you are making your cloth from scratch you will need to stitch a narrow edging lace following the drawn scallops using a narrow zig zag stitch then cut away the excess fabric from the back of the lace.*

—stitch No. 62 using a size-80 top stitch needle (oval satin stitch) length 12.0, width 6.0 and density 0.25 close to the scalloped edge of the cloth

—stitch No. 119 using a 120-wing needle (hem stitch scallop) length 20 width 7.5 on the inside edge of the above stitch (do not use paper as stabilizer)

—stitch No. 165 (satin stitch ball) width and length 3.0 density 0.25 following the outside edge of the previous scallop pivoting at the 'v' of the scallop.

NOTE: *If you are not used to stitching on inside curves, you may choose to use your single pattern button then pivot until you get used to what the stitch does next and can anticipate it so as not to distort the stitches.*

MOTIF EMBROIDERY

All motif embroidery requires melt-away or soluble stabilizer in the hoop sprayed with quilt basting spray for perfect placement (refer to page 14, stick-and-sew technique), Madeira pre-wound bobbin, size-80 top stitch needle and rayon 40 embroidery thread and Madeira Tanne/Cotona cotton thread.

10 Use the template marked positions to center your fabric under the needle and square in the hoop to embroider Lace1 over the vertical, horizontal and diagonal lines using the contrasting thread as color No. 1 and the white thread as color No. 2.

11 Lace9 is embroidered on the lines inbetween Lace1 so that the outside edge of the 'leaves' of the design just touch and sit on either side of the bottom drop of Lace1. Use the photo as a guide to color sequence (two colors only) in the embroidered motif.

NOTE: *If you have not achieved perfect placement with Lace1, then you can correct this by modifying the position of Lace9 so that it still just touches the outside edge of the drop on Lace1—this may mean that you have to change the angle of the design slightly but this will not matter in the overall look of the design when it is complete.*

12 Using the contrasting rayon thread embroider Lace19c in the center of the tablecloth.

CONNECTING BUILT IN STITCHES

13 Lace1 is connected at the widest points of the design with stitch No. 51 length 40.0 width 9.0 curving to the outside edge (should the gap between the designs slightly change then alter the length of this stitch to suit). On the outside edge of this scallop stitch No. 55 (shaped scallop) width and length 6.0, density 0.25 is stitched following the curve, single pattern button on and pivoting. On the top center of each of the above scalloped stitches, stitch No. 165, width and length 3.0, density 0.25, single pattern button is stitched then the connecting stitches clipped.

14 Using the 120-wing needle and stitch No. 112 (hem stitch) width 2.5 length 3.0, stitch around the outside edge of Lace9. This is stitched so the hole punched by the needle follows the outside edge of the motifs and swings over the edge of the outside row of stitching connecting the 16 designs into one magnificent design. Join Lace9 by following around the edge of the drop from Lace1 to connect all designs.

15 Embroider Lace6 in each corner of the cloth on the marked positions using colors that best match those used to complete the cloth.

16 Remove the stabilizer from the back of the embroidered tablecloth following the technique for melt-away stabilizer on page 14, and the fabric marking lines either by spraying or washing the cloth. Then iron over a towel from the wrong side of the cloth.

LACE CURTAIN

This sheer curtain would grace any window being both decorative and functional allowing the light and breeze to filter through an open window while affording privacy. It is also a wonderful project to explore the creative lace designs found on the Pfaff Victorian Lace CD.

- *80cm x 1.87m (31½in x 70in) sheer curtain fabric for curtain*
- *23cm (9in) wide strip the width of the same curtain fabric for embroidery*
- *Romeo water-soluble stabilizer for embroidery*
- *Helmar's Sew Stable soluble stabilizer*
- *Madeira pre-wound bobbins*
- *Pfaff PC-Designer software*
- *Pfaff Creative memory card*
- *Pfaff Victorian Lace CD by Jenny Haskins*
- *Vellum (112gsm) tracing paper to print out templates*
- *MACHINE NEEDLES: size-80 embroidery needle*
- *MACHINE FEET: 08 multi-directional foot, normal sewing foot and clear-view freehand foot*
- *Water-soluble fabric-marking pen*
- *Long ruler*
- *Small sharp scissors*
- *General sewing requirements.*

PREPARATION

1 Mix sufficient amounts of Sew Stable (one part solution to two parts water) to completely immerse the curtain and embroidery fabric then hang in the shade to dry.

2 Press the above, making sure it is true to grain.

CONTINUOUS EMBROIDERY

All embroidery requires white Madeira rayon 40 thread, Madeira pre-wound bobbins, size-80 embroidery needle and the lace designs are all stitched in a monochrome (single color).

Transfer Lace14 and Lace14a to a Pfaff creative card using the PC-Designer software and the Pfaff Victorian Lace CD.

3 Refer to Splendor in Linen and Lace page 75 step 14 to embroider eight Lace14 over the sheer fabric strip using Romeo as a backing stabilizer, to be cut out for the curtain header.

4 Embroider four Lace14 in a continuous line over two layers of Romeo for stand-alone lace scalloped border. Six sets of four joined Lace14 are needed for the scallops around the bottom edge of the curtain.

5 Embroider six, Lace14a singly over two layers of Romeo for stand-alone flowers that sit on the joining point of the scallops and on either end of the curtain.

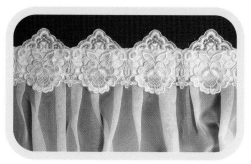

6 Refer to Romantic Net Wrap page 30 step 7 to cut out the eight embroidered motifs on the fabric strip for the curtain header (see above).

7 When stabilizer is removed from the six sets of four continuous Lace14 designs, cut the bars that connect the design. These bars are removed on either side of the small flower and the Fleur-de-lis shape (remove the small flower completely with its connecting bars) so the two large flowers can now be connected to one another and to the top of the Fleur-de-lis to form a lace shaped scallop for the bottom of the curtain.

8 Use the bar tack stitch No. 9 to connect flowers to each other and then another bar tack stitch to connect flowers to the top of the Fleur-de-lis (below).

Transfer Lace 9, Lace 10, Lace8, and Lace11 to a Pfaff creative card using the PC-Designer software and the Pfaff Victorian Lace CD. Use the Vellum (112gsm) tracing paper to print off placement templates for each of these designs referring to page 12 for markings and use of templates.

9 Leaving 5cm (2in) on either side of the fabric, divide the curtain fabric strip (its width) into six equal sections. Use the ruler and fabric-marking pen to rule vertical lines the length of the curtain to mark the divisions—mark top and bottom of curtain strip.

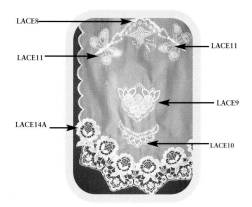

10 Working on bottom edge of the curtain, measure up 18cm (7in) on vertical lines and mark then rule a horizontal line that passes through this point and is parallel to the bottom of the curtain—center placement position for Lace9. Refer to instructions found inside the Victorian Lace CD to embroider Lace9 and Lace10 (with gap as in photo) on each line in the marked position. Use printed template for accurate placement of each design.

11 Measure up from the bottom edge of the curtain on the vertical lines 37cm (14½in) and mark then use the ruler and the fabric marking pen to draw a line through this point that is parallel to the bottom of the curtain. This is the center position for Lace8 fan. Embroider one on each marked position.

12 Use the template for Lace11 to position a butterfly on either side of Lace8 (fan) so it is angled down on either side of the fan, but faces up so the heart-shaped antennae are on either side of and in line with the fan's extremities. Repeat for all six fans.

SCALLOPED SIDES OF CURTAIN

Use the ruler and fabric-marking pen to draw a line down either side of the curtain that is parallel to and 5cm (2in) from the side edges of the curtain.

13 Use No. 8 multi-directional foot and paper as a stabilizer to embroider stitch No 201 (maxi scallop) down either side of the curtain. Remove paper then use a small sharp pair of scissors to cut around outside edge of the scallops close to the row of stitching.

APPLYING LACE SCALLOPS TO THE BOTTOM EDGE OF THE CURTAIN

14 Divide the embroidered curtain fabric width equally between each of the previous divisions made in step 9 to make 12 divisions. Mark each new division at the cut edge of the bottom of the curtain with a fabric-marking pen.

15 Use the fabric-marking pen and ruler to draw a line parallel to the bottom and 10cm (4in) up from it. Where this line intersects the first six divisons (of step 9) will be the meeting point of adjacent scallops over which Lace14a is positioned.

16 Pin then baste each curved lace section (flower facing up) to the bottom edge of the curtain starting 2.5cm (1in) from the cut edge. Place the bar tack between flowers 2 and 3 directly above the mark made in Step 14 with flowers 1 and 4 curving up towards the 10cm (4in) line and abutting the vertical lines of step 9. Refer to lower photo opposite.

TIP: *As this is machine-embroidered lace and is soft rayon, there is some give in the designs so they can be angled and adjusted to suit the curves.*

17 Repeat for the six scallops. Pin then baste Lace14a over the top of the meeting points of adjacent scallops and on either end of the curtain in line with the scalloped curtain sides.

18 Use the clear-view freehand foot and a narrow zigzag stitch to freehand along the top edge of the lace around the flowers, including Lace14a (step 17) to attach the lace to the bottom edge of the curtain.

19 Use a small sharp pair of scissors to cut away the fabric from the back of the lace close to the above row of stitching. Use warm soapy water to remove all stabilizer and fabric marking lines, then rinse, lay flat to dry and press.

20 Fold over a 2.5cm (1in) double hem at the top of the curtain and hem. Equally pleat up the top to measure the same length as the embroidered strip of fabric that sits over the header of the curtain.

21 With the lace facing down (flower down) and the scallops sitting over the top of the curtain, attach the lace to the top of the curtain with two rows of stitching, one close to the top of the curtain and the other 2.5cm (1in) down from and parallel to the first row of stitching. Attach hooks or casing as desired.

LACE TRIMMED
Linen

Sharman Dorcey, a southern belle, is a true Victorian lady who reflects this in her stores in Longview and Tyler TX, and every day life. This romantic bed linen mirrors the creativity of Sharman and her team, featuring lace combination designs to showcase the versatility of the Victorian Lace CD.

66

*T*here are several ways in which to embroider bed linen. If making your own from scratch, you cut the fabric and tailor the designs on the turn-back to fit, then stitch them from one side of the sheet to the other in which case the embroidery sequence is irrelevant.

On the other hand, should you choose to use ready-made sheets you may need to unpick the header on the sheet to embroider the edge, and in this case the embroidery sequence is important. A horizontal line should be drawn across the width of the sheet in a suitable position for the embroidery sequence. The first embroidery should be in the center front of the sheet then stitch one motif at a time alternately in each direction from the center out to the sides of the sheet until the entire edge is completed. If the last embroidery design doesn't end exactly on the edge of the sheet, angle it making a curved corner to fit it in. You may need to use two designs instead of one to accommodate the curve elegantly.

Pillowcases are treated in a similar way, unpicking the side seam/s of the pillowcase to embroider the edge, starting from the mid point and working to the edges in both directions as above.

MATERIALS

- White fabric of your choice or readymade bed linen
- Pfaff PC-Designer software
- Pfaff Creative memory card
- Pfaff Victorian Lace CD
- Vellum (112gsm) tracing paper for templates
- THREADS: Madeira white rayon 40 embroidery thread
- Madeira pre-wound bobbins
- Construction thread
- NEEDLES: size-80 embroidery needles and size-75 universal needles
- MACHINE FEET: clear-view freehand foot and normal sewing foot
- Ruler and water-fading fabric-marking pen
- Self-adhesive tear-away stabilizer
- Romeo water-soluble stabilizer
- Helmar's quilt basting spray
- Small sharp scissors
- General sewing requirements.

LACE TRIMMED *Linen*

NOTE: *All embroidery requires a size-80 embroidery needle; Madeira pre-wound bobbins and rayon 40 embroidery thread. Use the self-adhesive tear-away in the hoop for embroidery on fabric and Romeo water-soluble stabilizer for stand-alone lace.*

Pfaff PC-Designer software and the Pfaff Victorian Lace CD are used to transfer designs to a Pfaff Creative memory card. Print the designs on to tracing paper to be used as a template. Refer page 12 for the directions on the use of these templates.

The edge of the sheet is embroidered with Lace14, refer Splendor in Linen and Lace page 75 step 14 for how to embroider this design in a continuous line. You may choose to use the stick-and-sew technique (see page 14) under the edge of the fabric to make placement easier as this is not a stand-alone design. When embroidery is complete remove stabilizer then use a small sharp pair of scissors to cut away the outside edge of the scallops.

Scattered butterflies, either embroidered onto the fabric or freestanding then attached down the center of their bodies, are across the top of the sheet for added embellishment. (Lace3, Lace11, Lace 12, Lace13, Lace17, Lace17a and Lace17b)

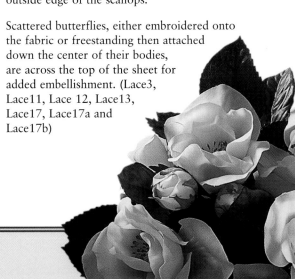

The edge of this pillowcase is trimmed with Lace16, stitched horizontally using the placement stitches and the template over Romeo soluble stabilizer, as this is a stand-alone continuous design. Stitch sufficient designs to go on both edges of the pillowcase. This is stitched on the edge of the front and back opening of the pillow slip following the shape of the lace, using a small zigzag stitch, then use a small sharp pair of scissors to cut the fabric away from the back of the lace.

Use the printed template for Lace5 and the photo as a guide to center two horizontal facing designs (one is a mirror image of the other) that touch at the center.

This pillow slip is trimmed with Lace10 so the designs just touch, over the self-adhesive tear-away using the printed template and the placement stitches to ensure perfect placement. As there are five designs on each edge of the pillowcase, stitch the center design on each opening edge (front and back) of the pillowslip first, then work from here to the outer edge alternately in both directions on both front and back for perfect alignment.

Two Lace15a and Lace15b are stitched centered horizontally, and facing each other using the photo as guide (mirror image style). Use the large hoop for this design, refer to page 100 for large hoop technique. Use your software to isolate the flower in the center of the second part of Lace19 and copy and paste then save to your blank card. Call this Flower19 and stitch out four times using Romeo stabilizer in the hoop as this is a stand-along design—you may choose to combine four in the one hoop placement. These lace flowers are then stitched on the inward point of each scallop. Add a seed pearl in the center of each flower with a hand-sewing needle.

This pillow slip is trimmed with Lace19 so the designs just touch. Use the stick-and-sew technique, the printed template and the placement stitches to ensure perfect placement. Use the printed template and the photo as a guide to position Lace1 and its mirror image centered in the front of the pillowcase so they meet at the wider side of the embroidery.

Use your software to isolate one of the flowers in Lace7 and copy and paste then save to your blank card. Call this Flower7 and stitch out three times over Romeo as a stand-along design—you may choose to combine three in the one hoop placement. These lace flowers are then stitched where the two designs meet. Stitch a seed pearl in the center of each with a hand-sewing needle.

SPLENDOR IN
Linen & Lace

*This simply scrumptious net, linen and lace bedspread is a
combination of creativity, talent, fine fabric, soft appealing color
and brilliant design—and it features every design in the
Pfaff Victorian Lace CD. My dear friend and fellow artist
Lucie took my concept, ran with it and the
result speaks for itself.*

70

LINEN & LACE
Bedspread

This is an advanced project involving the piecing techniques of a quilt but without backing or quilting-through because of the floaty, transparent nature of the lace and linen.

Look upon this as long-term but not daunting; with the right preparation it is very achievable, especially if you tackle and complete one block at a time.

The techniques are not difficult but do require dedication and concentration. Working on the premise that you only get out of a project what you are willing to put into it, this one is rather 'love intensive'. But the results are rewarding, self-endorsing and well worth the time.

MEASUREMENTS

Following the convention of quilting instructions, all measurements are in inches and yards.

Finished size of:

—bedspread (including the lace border) is 96in square

—center medallion is 37¾in square (tulle and linen)

—tulle square on point is 26½in square

—blocks, tulle and linen are 17in square

—sashing, linen with net squares at the corners, 3¾in wide

—borders, linen (before lace is attached), 6in wide

MATERIALS

FABRIC
- 3½yd x 36in wide ivory Swiss cotton tulle
- 4yd x 45in wide fine ivory linen

THREAD
- 27 x 1000m reels Madeira rayon 40 color No 1142 (light pink/brown) [5 reels for bed spread embroidery and 22 reels for edging lace]
- 4 x 1000m reels Madeira rayon 40 color No 1060 (beige)
- 1 x 1000m reel Madeira rayon 40 color No 1082 (cream)
- 3 x 150m reels Madeira Cotona 30 color No 1082 (cream)
- 2 x 200m reels Madeira Cotona 50 No 504 (cream) for pin tucking and embroidery
- Cream cotton thread for construction
- 33 Madeira pre-wound bobbins
- Pfaff PC-Designer software
- Pfaff bank memory card
- Pfaff Victorian Lace CD
- Pfaff large hoop
- 30 sheets of vellum (112gsm) tracing paper to print off templates
- NEEDLES: 75/11 embroidery needles, 3.0/80-twin needle, 1.6/70-twin needle, 120-wing needle, 70 universal needle
- MACHINE FEET: Open-toe embroidery, 7-groove cording foot and cording blade, 6mm cording foot (used to give a 6mm gap between the pin tucks and for centering and embroidering down the 6mm gap), hoop embroidery foot, ¼-inch foot (for seaming if not overlocking seams)
- Romeo soluble stabilizer for motif embroidery and some built-in stitch embroidery
- Photocopy paper for under appliquéd lace motifs and built-in satin stitches
- Water soluble marking pen
- 1 bottle Helmar's liquid stabilizer
- 1 bottle fray stopper
- Lace pins
- Quilting ruler, Olfa cutting mat and rotary cutter
- Small curved scissors for cutting around embroidery
- Spray starch
- Protractor
- 18in square sheet of white paper
- General sewing requirements

NOTE: See *layout diagram on pattern sheet*

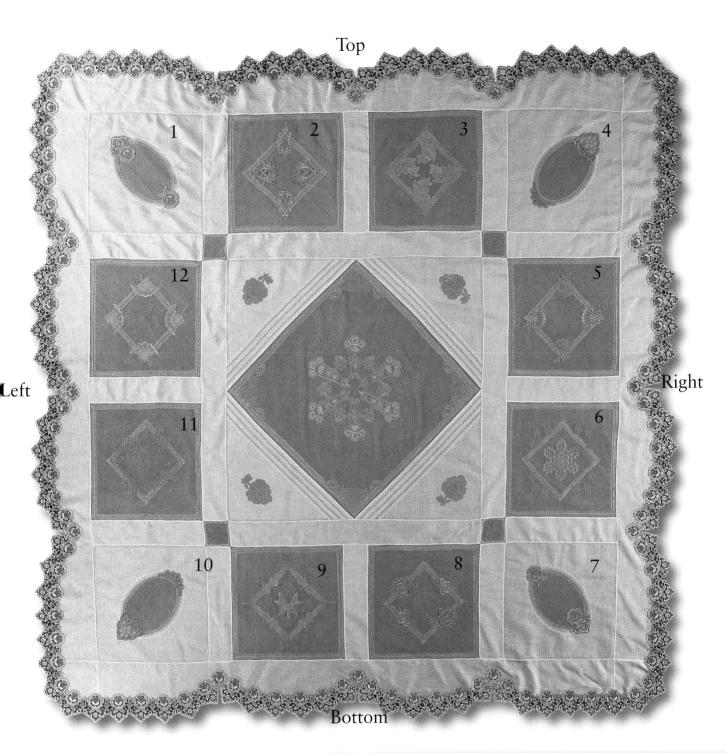

Top

Left

Right

1   2   3   4

12   5

11   6

10   9   8   7

Bottom

PREPARATION

CUTTING

1 Pre shrink fabric by washing in warm soapy water and then stretch true to grain and dry in the shade.

2 When nearly dry, press with a steam iron, making sure the fabric is true to grain, especially the cotton net tulle.

NOTE: *Extra fabric is allowed for shrinkage caused by embroidery and hooping.*

3 Use the Olfa mat, quilting ruler and rotary cutter to cut from the linen:

—four, 18in square blocks (one in each corner of the quilt)

— two, 22½in squares (cut later into 4 triangles for center block)

—four, 39in x 4¼in strips for center medallion borders

—12, 17½in x 4¼in strips for sashing between blocks

—four, 80in x 6in strips for outer border

—four, 6½in squares for border corners

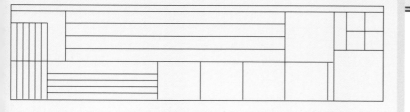

4 From the cotton net tulle:
—one, 29in square for center square on point

—eight, 18in squares. (You may find that after pre shrinking, the width of the net is less than 36in, halve the width, which gives close to 18in.)

—mark four 5in squares, using water-soluble fabric-marking pen, on remaining fabric. **NOTE:** *Do not cut out at this time—as squares are for small hoop placement and it is easier if they are left uncut. After these squares are embroidered they are cut to 4½in squares to be used in the center medallion border corners.*

— mark, four ovals using template from pattern sheet, allowing an extra ½in of tulle around each oval as a seam allowance when cutting out.

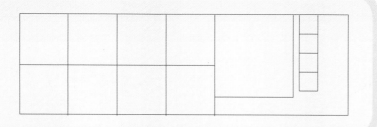

STABILIZING FABRIC

NOTE: *As these designs are very stitch intense and the fabrics fine, it is of utmost importance that the fabric is stabilized and the correct backing stabilizer used for embroidery to ensure the best results. Please read the following carefully and follow the instructions.*

5 Prior to embroidery, stabilize all fabric pieces that have been cut out, including the leftover pieces of tulle, using Helmar's liquid fabric stabilizer. A solution of one part stabilizer with two parts water works best. Dry flat in the shade then press taking care not to distort the tulle squares.

6 For hoop embroidery, two layers of water-soluble stabilizer such as Romeo were used to embroider lace. When embroidering over the cotton net tulle or linen using one layer of Romeo , simplify the process by applying basting spray to the hooped Romeo and then treat it as self-adhesive stabilizer and place the fabric on the stabilizer rather than hooping the fabric. This is referred to as the stick-and-sew technique.

7 For built-in stitch embroidery use either tear-away, photocopy paper or Romeo under 9mm satin stitches only.

8 No stabilizer was used under stitch No 27.

THREADS AND NEEDLES

9 All hoop motif embroidery requires water soluble stabilizer in the hoop either sprayed with a basting spray or with the fabric in the hoop (whichever you prefer), rayon embroidery thread, Madeira pre-wound bobbins and size-75/11 embroidery needles.

10 The lace designs from the Pfaff Victorian Lace CD need to be downloaded on to a blank memory card using the PC-Designer software either through the machine or the Card Station. These designs are too memory intense to be fitted on one card so the designs will need to be deleted when sewn out so there is room for the next design.

11 All embroidery designs need to be printed at a 1.1 ratio onto the vellum, (112gsm) tracing paper to ensure simple and accurate placement. My unique placement stitches are built into every embroidery design to ensure perfect placement, so make sure you read the instructions that come with the CD. Print out all designs from the Victorian Lace CD and you'll have permanent transparent placement templates. Refer to page 12 for using templates.

PREPARATION EMBROIDERY

12 On each of the marked-out 5in squares on the tulle, embroider Lace3 using the pink/brown thread and positioning the butterfly on the diagonal in the center of each block.

13 On the leftover tulle embroider:
—four, Lace2 in beige thread

—two, Lace10 in pink/brown thread and beige thread

—two, Lace9 in pink/brown thread and beige thread

—two, Lace14a in pink/brown thread

—two, Lace14b in pink/brown thread.

The stick-and-sew method is best used with the stabilizer to get the most out of the fabric and eliminates hooping the fabric.

14 LACE FOR THE EDGE OF THE QUILT:

Note that the 104 Lace14 and 12 Lace14a (stitched out singly) are embroidered with the pink/brown thread in a continuous line using two layers of Romeo water-soluble stabilizer only as these designs stand alone. Use my positioning stitches for accurate placement of these designs and joining of Lace14.

—stitch design in the default direction

—stitch the first design Lace14 and before removing the design from the hoop use a water-fading pen to mark the position of the last two jump stitches (as with large hoop) and draw around the inside edge of the top of hoop

—use the vellum (112gsm) tracing paper template to position the next design, making sure to mark the vertical and horizontal lines of the design to align with the notches on the hoop

—re-hoop the stabilizer so the inside hoop line (drawn above) sits on the inside edge of the inner hoop at rear of the hoop (the side closest to you) and the centering lines on the stabilizer align with the placement notches marked on the hoop

—press the 'pattern start' key so the needle swings to the start of the pattern—the first three stitches are placement jump stitches, 1 and 3 correspond to the last placement jump stitches that are marked with the water-fading pen (2 sits on the Y)

—press the foot control twice so the needle swings to the second and third placement marked position

NOTE: *To join two Lace14s, the needle* **must** *swing into the exact position where it stitched the last two stitches of the previous design. This ensures that the design matches and stitches out as 'yardage'. Being patient and accurate pays off and in no time this technique becomes quite easy, so persevere—the results are worth it.*

Lace embroidery can be done over a long period. If you have two machines (one embroidery and one for sewing such as a Pfaff 2140, 7570, or 7560 and a 7550) do the built-in stitching while the other machine stitches the lace. Sew lace when you are doing something else at home so that your machine is continually sewing. When leaving the machine unattended, engage the half speed button.

Refer to page 14 for the removal of soluble stabilizer.

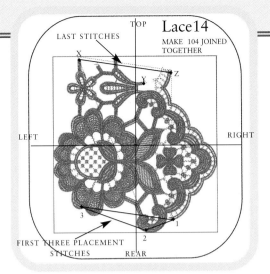

TO JOIN LACE14 AS A CONTINUOUS PIECE, MARK WITH PEN POINTS 'Z' AND 'X' AND INSIDE HOOP AT 'TOP', RE-HOOP THE STABILIZER WITH CENTERING LINES FOR THE SECOND MOTIF ALIGNED WITH HOOP NOTCHES AND TOP HOOP MARK AT REAR OF HOOP. PRESS 'PATTERN START' AND THE NEW POINTS 1 AND 3 WILL ALIGN WITH THE 'Z' AND 'X' OF THE FIRST MOTIF.

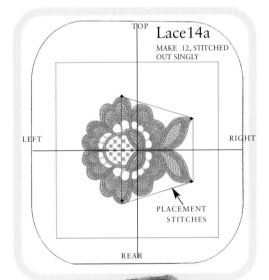

CENTER MEDALLION

Center block net tulle square set on point

MOTIF EMBROIDERY

15 On the 29in tulle square, use the fabric-marking pen and a ruler to draw a centered 26½in square. (This square will be referred to as a diamond from here on, as the square is set on point and thus looks like a diamond shape.) Draw another line ¾in inside the first diamond. Mark the top and bottom of the diamond.

16 Use the fabric-marking pen and the ruler to draw a diagonal line from the top corner to the bottom corner of the diamond, then find the center of this line and mark this position.

17 Using a protractor, mark further lines at 60° intervals from the center of the diagonal line. On these placement lines measure 6⅛in from the center and mark for the center position of the first half of the design Lace15a. These are the placement lines for the first six center lace motifs Lace15a and 15b. **REFER TO PAGE 100 FOR DIRECTIONS ON USING THE LARGE HOOP.**

18 Lace15a and 15b are printed out in two segments on the vellum (112gsm) tracing paper, as they require the large hoop. Overlap and tape them to form one design (see pattern sheet diagram). Use this template and positions marked in the center of the net square to position then sew the first six motifs using pink/brown and cream thread; refer to the photo as a guide to sequence used. (I think you will find it easier to use the stick-and-sew technique rather than hooping the fabric when using the large hoop.)

19 Use your software to delete the connecting bars from the end of Lace19c then print out this template and position it 4½in from the center of the diamond between Lace15 so that the sides just meet. Use the photo as guide to color, direction and position of Lace19c. Use the 120-hoop and the stick-and-sew technique (page 14) to stitch out these designs.

NOTE: *The corner lace embroidery motifs are sewn over the built-in stitching around the edge of the diamond. Sew these rows of stitching next.*

BUILT-IN STITCH EMBROIDERY

All built-in stitch embroidery requires 75/11 embroidery needle, open-toe foot and Madeira pre-wound bobbins. No stabilizer behind stitch No. 27 but photocopy paper is used behind stitch No. 16.

20 Using the ¾in line on the outside edge of the diamond as a guide for the edge of the open-toe foot and cream rayon 30 thread, embroider stitch No. 27 length 20, width 9.0 around the diamond, then sew another row the other side of the guideline.

21 Embroider along the ¾in guideline using stitch No. 16 width 2.5 density 0.6 in pink/brown thread.

22 Use two reels of rayon 40 thread, 3.0/80 twin needle (twin needle button engaged) select stitch No 112, length 3.0 width 2.0 centering the stitching over the previous row of satin stitching so that this row of stitching runs along either side of the satin stitching.

NOTE: *These rows of embroidery are repeated on the center and around the edge of all the tulle blocks.*

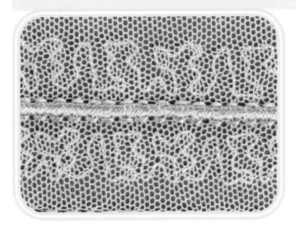

23 Center the template for Lace7 in each inside corner of the embroidered diamond so one flower sits in the corner and the leaves just meet the row of twin needle stitching on either side of the corner and sits over stitch No. 27 embroidery. Stitch these out in each corner using pink/brown thread.

24 Use the template for Lace19a to position this design on either side of Lace7 so it is slightly angled from Lace7 to the twin needle stitching, using the same threads that were used in the center designs and the photo as guide to direction (see photo at left).

25 Wash out soluble stabilizer and marking lines in warm soapy water and lay flat to dry in the shade. Press with spray starch, trim to a 27in square and put to one side.

LINEN CORNER TRIANGLES

Pin tucks and embroidery on the corner triangles
26 On each 22½in linen square use the fabric-marking pen and ruler to draw the following lines:

—a diagonal line from one corner to the other.

—two lines 1½in either side of this line.

NOTE: *The center diagonal line is the cutting line to make a total of four triangles with embroidery along the diagonal edge of each. Instructions will be given for embroidery for one edge to be repeated on all four edges. Do not cut yet.*

27 Use two reels of cream Cotona 50 thread, 1.6/70 twin-needle, 7 groove cording foot and blade to sew the first row of pin tucking along both of the lines either side of the center diagonal line. Sew two rows of pin tucks on either side of the center diagonal line extending in the direction of each corner.

NOTE: *All pin tucks and embroidery are sewn on either side of the diagonal line, extending in the direction of each rightangle corner.*

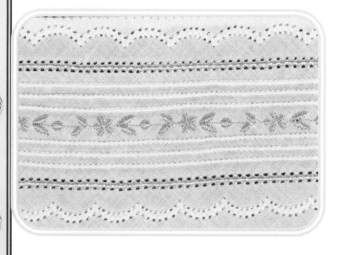

TIP: *Sew pin tucks in opposite directions to reduce stretch in the fabric as it is sewn on the bias.*

28 Change to the 6mm-pin tuck/cording foot and blade to sew the third and forth rows of pin tucking—this leaves a 6mm gap between the fourth and fifth pin tucks which has a decorative stitch sewn down the middle.

29 Change back to the 7-groove cording foot to sew two more rows of pin tucks, extending to the corner giving a total of six pin tucks, with a 6mm gap between the third and fourth pin tuck.

30 Repeat the above on the other side of the centerline and the second 22½in linen-block.

NOTE: *The Pfaff 7570 sewing machine has the ability not only to mirror designs, but also to axel (flip or flop) them as well on most stitches. There are some however that will not do this in the normal manner. To overcome this you can either use the software, or go to a 'P'-Memory, import the desired stitch through 'rom' then the stitch can be axeled (flip flopped). This stitch can be sewn out directly through the 'P'-memory or combined in the 'M'-memory with other stitches and this is what has been done to achieve the design sewn down the center of the 6mm gap in the pin tucks.*

31 Create a stitch sequence to be sewn down the 6mm gap between the center pin tucks:

—import stitch No. 123 into a 'P'-memory through 'rom'

—open an 'M'-memory and combine the following:
Stitch No. 123 from the 'P'-memory length normal width 6.0 density 0.25, stitch No. 136 length 9.0 width 6.0, stitch No 123 from the 'P'-memory length normal width 6.0 density 0.25 axeled (flip flopped) and finally stitch No 165 width and length 4.0 density 0.25.

32 Use the 6mm pin tuck foot, 75/11 embroidery needle, rayon 40 embroidery thread (pink/brown color), Madeira pre-wound bobbin and photocopy paper at the back of the embroidery to act as a stabilizer to stitch the above stitch sequence, stored in an 'M'-memory, down the 6mm gap in the center of the four sets of pin tucks on the two linen blocks.

33 Change to the open-toe foot, then use the edge of the foot along the pin tuck nearest the corner as a guide, to sew stitch No. 16 width 2.5 density 0.6 either side of each set of pin tucks. Repeat for the second block.

34 Change to the 120-wing needle, cream rayon 40 thread and select stitch

No. 111 length 3.0 width 3.0, to sew over the previous row of stitching. Repeat on the edge of the pin tuck nearest the center diagonal line.

35 Change thread to cream Cotona 50 and still using the 120-wing needle, and the edge of the foot as a guide along the previous row of stitching, to sew stitch No. 119 length 22 width 7.5, repeat on the other side of the pin tuck and stitch sequence to complete the design. Repeat on all sets of pin tucks.

CENTER MEDALLION

36 Use the rotary cutter, Olfa mat and quilting ruler to cut down the center diagonal line of the two squares (making four triangles.) Spray with water to remove any fabric-marking pen lines, then press.

NOTE: *After the seams have been joined using the ¼-inch foot and a straight stitch, they are neatened either by using a serger and a narrow three-thread overlock over both edges of the seam together, using a fine thread (as we have) or a narrow 'roll and whip' using a zig zag stitch. Before joining, and at the completion of each section of the quilt, trim the sides to the directed size prior to sewing the seams and neatening them.*

37 Attach the corner triangle to each side of the center diamond with construction thread, size-70 universal needle and the ¼-inch foot. Finish the seams in your preferred way then press seams towards the linen (this ensures the seams are not seen through the cotton net tulle.)

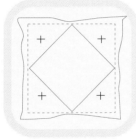

CENTER MEDALLION

38 Use the open-toe foot, 75/11 embroidery needle, pink/brown thread, Madeira pre-wound bobbin and stitch No. 112 length 3.0 width 2.0, to sew over the seams so the stitch swings from the net to the linen, thus ensuring the seam sits flat over the linen.

NOTE: *All seams are treated in this way.*

39 Mark linen corners so they are square and in line with the points on the center diamond using a fabric marking pen and ruler then 'square' up the central 'block' to measure 38¼in.

40 Position and tack the four stitched-out Lace2 designs in the center of each linen triangle on either side of the center diamond.

NOTE: *Do not trim tulle from the outside edge of the embroidery design until you have completed the two rows of stitching to appliqué the design in place.*

41 Appliqué the motifs in place using matching thread, an open-toe foot, size-75/11 embroidery needle, Madeira pre-wound bobbin and stitch No. 02 (zigzag) width 1.0 density 0.4, pivoting around curves with the needle down.

42 From the right side of the fabric, using a small sharp pair of scissors carefully cut the tulle away from the outside edge of the embroidered motif.

43 Change to the 120-wing needle, engage the twin needle button to sew stitch No. 112 length 3.0 width 2.0, following and close to the edge of the motif.

44 Carefully, and remembering less is best, (use a pin to pierce the top of the bottle, do not cut the tip off), apply fray stopper to the inner edge of the linen close to the embroidery. Let dry, then use a small sharp pair of scissors such as duckbill scissors to cut away the fabric from behind the appliqué. Repeat for all four appliqués.

CENTER MEDALLION BORDERS

45 Use the ¼in-foot, construction thread, size 70-universal needle and a straight stitch to attach the top and bottom borders (39in x 4½in strips) to the center medallion.

NET BUTTERFLY SQUARE

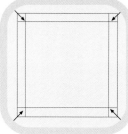

CENTER MEDALLION
SHOWING DIRECTION
BUTTERFLIES ARE FACING

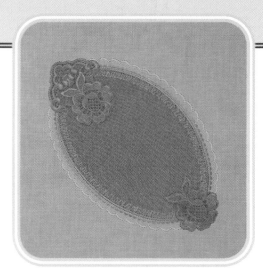

BLOCKS 1 & 7

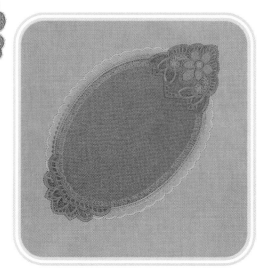

BLOCKS 4 & 10

46 Attach a net butterfly square to each end of the two remaining border fabric strips then attach these to either side of the center medallion taking care to match all seamlines and to have the butterflies facing inwards.

47 Press seams over the linen.

48 On the 4½in net squares on the corners of the center medallion select the open-toe foot, size 75/11 embroidery needle, Madeira pre-wound bobbin, cream rayon 30 thread and stitch No. 14 length 2.0 width 7.5, to stitch around the outside edge of the square close to the seamline. Select stitch No. 136 length 12 width 9.0 single pattern button engaged, in each corner with beige rayon 40 thread to sew a flower in each corner of the net squares.

49 On the four linen triangle corners of the center medallion select the above foot, needle and bobbin to sew stitch No. 50 length 10 width 5.0, using gray rayon 40 thread close to the seamline.

TIP: *Start from the corner and sew to embroidery on the diagonal edge of the fabric, manipulating the stitch so a pattern is completed on each end of the row of embroidery.*

50 Repeat step 38 around the border seams of the center medallion. This completes the medallion

QUILT BLOCKS

Corner Linen blocks with oval net insert.
Blocks 1, 4, 7 and 10.

NOTE: *All embroidery requires either an open-toe foot or a motif embroidery foot, rayon embroidery thread, Madeira pre-wound bobbins and size 75/11 embroidery needles unless otherwise stated.*

51 Fold each block on the diagonal from corner to corner then press. Use the oval template from the pattern sheet, position in the center of the block matching the lines and center position on the template to those on the block then draw around the oval with a fabric-marking pen.

52 Place net tulle oval over the oval drawn on the linen then use a straight stitch and construction thread to stitch around the two aligned ovals making sure the net and linen are flat and smooth.

53 Using pink/brown rayon thread select stitch No. 16 width 3.0 density 0.6 to sew on the marked oval line.

54 From the right side of the fabric, using a small sharp pair of scissors carefully cut the tulle from the outside edge of the satin stitching close to the stitch line, being careful not to clip the stitching threads.

TIP: *Start and finish at one end of the oval as it doesn't matter if the stitches do no match up, as this area will be cut away later.*

55 Using cream rayon 40 thread and a 120-wing needle sew stitch No. 111 length 3.0 width 3.0 over the first row of embroidery.

56 On the wrong side of the linen inside the embroidered oval shape close to the embroidery, apply fray stopper sparingly to the linen (as for the appliqué in the corners of the center medallion), allow to dry before cutting the linen away from the net oval.

57 On the linen, using the edge of your foot on the previous row of embroidery as a guide, sew stitch No. 60 length 6.0 width 4.0 density 0.25, around the outside edge of the net oval on the linen.

58 Continuing on the linen and using the edge of the foot as a guide, select the 120-wing needle and cream Cotona thread, to sew stitch No. 119 length 22 width 7.5, around the outside edge of the previous row of stitching.

59 On the inside edge of the net tulle using cream rayon 30 thread, sew stitch No. 27 (length 20 width 9.0) with the edge of the foot as a guide on the row of satin stitching around the outside edge of the net oval.

60 Use water in a spray bottle to remove any fabric-marking lines, then press. **DO NOT** rinse yet, as the stabilizer is still needed.

61 Press in the diagonal corner-to-corner line through the long axis of the oval. This line is used to position accurately the embroidery motifs to be appliquéd.

REPEAT ON ALL FOUR CORNER LINEN BLOCKS.

62 Position embroidered lace motifs (Lace9 and Lace10, Lace14a and Lace14b) using the photo as a guide to positioning. It is advisable to baste in place to ensure accuracy.

63 Refer to steps 41 to 44 to appliqué the embroidered motifs in place and complete the four corner blocks.

NET LACE BLOCKS

Block 2, 3, 5, 6, 8, 9, 11 and 12

All these blocks have similarities, which will be treated as one, with individual embroideries being treated separately according to the numbered block.

64 Take each lace block and fold in half on the vertical and horizontal pressing each fold separately.(**FIG. A**)

65 Use a fabric-marking pen to mark a position that is 5½in from center on all lines. (**FIG. B**)

66 Use the fabric-marking pen to connect these points to form a diamond (square on point).

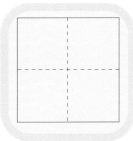

FIGURE A   FIGURE B

67 Refer to steps 20 to 22 on page 77 as used on the net in the center of the quilt, for embroidery sequence, again using the marked diamond as a guide for the edge of the foot.

EMBROIDER ALL EIGHT BLOCKS IN LIKE MANNER.

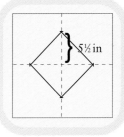

BLOCK NO 2

Use the vellum (112gsm) tracing paper templates and the photo as a guide to colors used and positioning to stitch the following embroidery motifs in place around the embroidered diamond:

—two, Lace1: over top and bottom corners of diamond

—two, Lace5: sitting inside the diamond on either side

BLOCK NO 3

Use the Vellum (112gsm) tracing paper templates and the photo as a guide to colors used and positioning to stitch the following embroidery motifs in place around the embroidered diamond:

—four, Lace16: centered on the diagonal in each corner of the diamond facing inwards

—four, Lace17: small butterfly only, centered at each corner of the diamond

—four, Lace17b enlarged (74.7mm x 41.1mm): larger butterfly centered between the smaller butterflies on each side of the diamond

BLOCK NO 5

Use the vellum (112gsm) tracing paper templates and the photo as a guide to colors used and positioning to stitch the following embroidery motifs in place around the embroidered diamond:

—four, Lace4: centered straight over each corner of the embroidered diamond

BLOCK NO 6

Use the tracing paper templates and the photo as a guide to colors used and positioning to stitch the following embroidery motifs in place around the embroidered diamond:

—one, Lace20c: round lace center piece, centered in the embroidered diamond

—six, Lace20a: oval-shaped lace end piece equally spaced around Lace20b in the center of the

embroidered diamond using protractor and 60° angles.

Use the software and Lace20c to create the three flowers that are centered on each side of the square. The flower is the center of Lace21c and should be hi-lighted then cut and pasted into a new screen to create a new design with one flower centered and a flower on either side slightly lower than the center and equal on either side. Refer to the photo as a guide.

—the above flowers, four times, one set, centered on the outside edge of each side of the embroidered diamond.

BLOCK NO 8

Use the tracing paper templates and the photo as a guide to colors used and positioning to stitch the following embroidery motifs in place around the embroidered diamond:

—four Lace6: antique lace flower centered over each side of the embroidered diamond with the flower facing to the outside

BLOCK NO 9

Use the tracing paper templates and the photo as a guide to colors used and positioning to stitch the following embroidery motifs in place around the embroidered diamond:

—one Lace12: large antique butterfly centered in the embroidery diamond

—four, Lace11: antique moth centered over the embroidered diamond on each side

—four, Lace13 x 4 (enlarged 75.2mm x 55.1mm): antique butterfly with the butterfly centered over each corner so the heart-shaped head and antennae are sitting inside the embroidered diamond on each corner.

BLOCK NO 11

Use the tracing paper templates and the photo as a guide to colors used and positioning to stitch the following embroidery motifs in place around the embroidered diamond:

—four, Lace19: antique lace centered over each side of the embroidered diamond

BLOCK NO 12

Use the tracing paper templates and the photo as a guide to colors used and positioning to stitch the following embroidery motifs in place around the embroidered diamond:

—one, Lace 17A: large lace butterfly, centered in the embroidered diamond

—four, Lace8: lace fan, centered over each corner (facing in) of the embroidered diamond

TO COMPLETE THE BEDSPREAD

SQUARING THE NET LACE BLOCKS

With warm soapy water remove all stabilizer and water-soluble fabric marking pen lines—you may need to leave this soaking for around 30 minutes before rinsing in cold water. You may need to do this several times until the water is clear. Lay flat in the shade to dry then press over a towel making sure not to distort the net or the embroidery.

'Shaping' the blocks is made easier by using the 'template' on the pattern sheet—you may choose to use this one or trace one onto another piece of paper to save your pattern sheet.

The tulle blocks can now be laid over the template to center the embroidery, then use a ruler and a water-soluble fabric-marking pen to draw the 17½in square cutting lines. Use the rotary cutter, quilting ruler and Olfa mat to square the blocks and trim excess tulle from around the edge of each block.

JOINING THE BLOCKS

NOTE: *The ¼-inch foot, size 70 universal needle and construction thread is used to piece the quilt using the serger and a three thread overlock stitch to neaten the seams which are always pressed away from the net tulle over the linen.*

The blocks are sewn together into 4 rows. Refer to the photo of the quilt (page 73) to determine the direction the block is facing in the quilt before joining the block rows.

Row No 1—top of quilt
Join blocks 1, 2, 3 and 4 together with the 17½in x 4¼in linen sashing strips between each block

Row No 2—bottom of quilt
Join blocks 7, 8, 9 and 10 together with the 17½in x 4¼in linen sashing strips between each block.

Row 3—right hand side of the quilt
Join blocks 5 and 6 together with a 17½in x 4¼in linen sashing strip

Row 4—left hand side of the quilt
Join blocks 11 and 12 together with a 17½in x 4¼in linen sashing strip

JOINING THE ROWS TO THE CENTER MEDALLION

Join rows three and four to either side of the center medallion then rows one and two to the top and bottom of the center medallion taking care to match all seams and checking to see that the blocks are facing in the correct direction.

JOINING THE OUTER BORDERS

Join a 6½in linen square to each end of two of the 80in x 6½in linen border strips. Join the remaining two border strips to either side of the quilt then the longer strips to the top and bottom of the quilt.

EMBROIDERING INSIDE THE NET LACE SQUARES

Using the edge of the open-toe foot on the inside seamlines as a guide to repeat steps 20 to 22 around the inside of each net lace square block. Refer to block photo as a guide.

STITCHING OVER THE SEAMS

Stitch No. 112 length 3.0, width 2.0 using pink/brown rayon thread is sewn over all seamlines as for the center medallion in step 38, stopping and starting at the embroidered net squares on the border strips around the center medallion.

On the four linen corner squares stitch No. 50 is sewn on the inside of stitch No. 112 length 10 width 6, in the same manner as the triangles in the center medallion, see step 49.

The four small net lace squares with the embroidered butterfly in the center are treated separately as the seams at the back must be twisted so the seams go over the linen not the lace, then held in place with the above stitch swinging from the net over the linen to hold the seam flat.

LACE EDGE

The making of this lace is dealt with in detail in step 14. Lace border is made using Lace14 and Lace14a.

If you have not managed to embroider your lace motifs consecutively, then join the following taking care to continue the scalloped edge along the bottom of the lace and ensure the lace joins at the side of each flower with the connecting struts; you may have to fudge a bit here if necessary:

—eight lengths of 6 x Lace14 joined together for scallops

—four, lengths of 12 x Lace14 joined together for corners

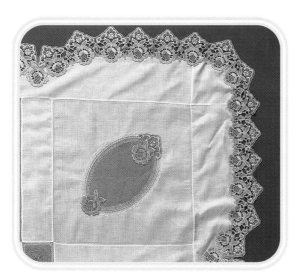

The lace is shaped for the corners and the scallops on the sides of the quilt in the normal way you would shape lace into a curve and to go around corners.

Using the photos as a guide to cut out the top bars between small and large flowers to allow them to curve. Extra needs to be cut out between the motifs to make the corners sit flat—again use the photo as a guide.

Re-join the lace where cut using matching thread and a narrow closed up zigzag stitch.

As this lace is soft and can stretch, it can be shaped and manipulated around curves easily.

CORNERS

Center the join of the two flowers over each corner, and pin, then measure 24½in from each corner on either side of the corner then pin the corner lace in place making it fit. This mark is centered in the sashing strip on each side of each corner block.

SIDES

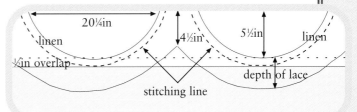

Center the two lace scallops on each side of the quilt and pin in place using the diagram above as a guide.

Pin, then baste the lace units in place with a ½in overlap of the inner edge of the scallop curve over the linen. Leave the single motifs until later.

Appliqué the lace to the linen along the inner edge in the same manner used to appliqué the motifs to the linen blocks using matching thread and a narrow satin stitch following the outside edge of the lace motifs.

Position, pin and baste a single motif over each scallop join—three on each side of the quilt—then appliqué as above.

Remove basting from all lace.

Check to see that all joins in the bottom edge of the lace have been sewn together with a matching narrow satin stitch.

From the wrong side of the quilt, carefully apply fray stopper to the linen where it will be trimmed away. Allow the fray stopper to dry then trim away the unwanted linen edge below the lace border.

Remove any marking lines and press.

DIVINE DECADENCE

Gloria McKinnon and the team from Anne's Glory Box explore the possibilities of hand beading, embroidery and lavishly decorated frames to enhance these turn-of-the century silk prints aptly named Veronica (on the left) and Jeanette. This type of handwork typifies the pastimes of the Victorian Lady even though the fashions represented here herald a new era. These silk prints can be obtained in a kit form.

SEE PAGE 102.

93

LADIES IN WAITING

Gloria and her team certainly have a winning way with needle and thread and here they demonstrate a variation on the theme from the previous pages with brilliant color and clever design. Handwork is the perfect answer when it is not possible to take your machine with you. It wiles away the hours, soothes the soul and the results are glorious. These ladies in waiting, Dolores (left) and Felicity, are available in kit form.

SEE PAGE 102

LAVISH
Lace Fan

❦❧

Although this looks like it's one hundred years old, in fact this fan was my first exciting venture into the Victorian Lace designs when they were sent to me not long ago. The designs are stitched over cotton net tulle and then I used the hand-painted lace technique from VICTORIAN PANSIES *to color the lace with commercial dyes.*

T used the struts of an old fan.

MATERIALS

- 25cm x 2.30m (10in) cotton net tulle (90in) wide
- Inexpensive plastic fan
- Pfaff PC-Designer software
- Pfaff Creative memory card
- Pfaff Victorian Lace CD
- Machine needles: size-80 embroidery needle
- Romeo water-soluble stabilizer
- Thread: Madeira rayon 40 embroidery thread in a pale color
- Madeira pre-wound bobbins
- 30cm (12in) beaded floral trim in shades of purples and pinks to match the dyed lace
- Commercial fabric dyes and small paint brushes
- Potassium permanganate
- Antique beaded tassel
- 450 craft glue
- General sewing requirements

PREPARATION

1 Cut a 25cm x 50cm (10in x 20in) rectangle from the cotton net tulle then use a fabric marking pen to draw a half circle with a 23cm (9in) radius. This is to cover the fan struts.

2 The remaining net fabric will be used for embroidery.

EMBROIDERY

3 Use the Pfaff PC-Designer software and Victorian Lace CD to transfer Lace1 and Lace19 to a Pfaff Creative card. All embroidery requires rayon 40 embroidery thread, size-80 embroidery needle and a Madeira pre-wound bobbin.

4 The embroidery is done over one layer of cotton net tulle and one layer of Romeo water-soluble stabilizer.

5 Embroider the following:
—seven, Lace1
—five, Lace19 in a continuous line

6 When embroidery is complete, wash out the stabilizer then use a small sharp pair of scissors to carefully cut out each Lace1 and to cut around the outside edge of the continuous Lace19.

7 Refer to Techniques Directory on page 100 for antique dyeing and hand painted lace technique. Use a dirty olive green and deep purple, finishing with the potassium permanganate to give an antique finish. Use the photo as a guide to colors used.

8 Dye the half circle of cotton net tulle using the dirty olive green color.

9 Allow lace motifs and net to dry flat before ironing with a hot steam iron over a towel from the wrong side. The net should be ironed flat and true to grain.

10 Use the 450 craft glue to glue the struts of the fan evenly spaced at the back of the net half circle,

turning the raw fabric edges on the side of the net under on the sides of the fan. Trim excess fabric from around the top and center from the front of the fan.

11 Glue the purple edging Lace19 around the top of the fan covering the raw net edge and extending over it using the photo as a guide to the direction of the lace.

12 Glue Lace1 in between every second strut of the fan so the narrow section of the design is at the bottom and the wider section sits over the edging lace.

13 Glue the beaded lace trim around the bottom edge of the lace tulle to cover the raw edge then glue or tie the beaded tassel to the bottom of the fan to complete this delicate fan.

PICTURE OF
Elegance

*P*aintings and prints from the Victorian era are an endless source of inspiration for 21st century embroiderers. These delightful ladies are in Carol Cree's range of kits and she has embellished them with hand embroidery, beads and trims. Try using your machine embroidery stitches to replicate Carol's handwork. See page 102 for credits.

TECHNIQUES
Directory

**ANTIQUE DYEING OF LACE
USING POTASSIUM PERMANGANATE:**
see *Victorian Pansies* page 82.

HAND PAINTED LACE:
see *Victorian Pansies* page 83.

MITERED CORNERS:
see *Victorian Pansies* page 89 and
Victorian Roses page 95.

QUILT BINDING:
see *Victorian Pansies* page 90 and
Victorian Roses page 96.

**STIPPLE-QUILTING/FREEHAND
EMBROIDERY:**
see *Victorian Pansies* page 85 and
Victorian Roses page 85.

MAKING A TWISTED CORD:
see *Victorian Roses* page 97.

**USING SELF-ADHESIVE TEAR-AWAY
IN HOOP:**
see *Victorian Pansies* page 86 and
Victorian Roses page 12.

Techniques

USE OF THE LARGE HOOP

These instructions only apply to the the Pfaff 7570, 7560 and 7562 machines. Refer to pages 20 and 21 in the instruction book that comes with the large hoop; this is a valuable reference.

In these instructions, the 'top' of the hoop is the narrow side furthest away from you when you stitch (on the far side of the needle), the 'rear' is the other narrow side which is closest to you, the left is on your left and the right is on your right and is the long side with the adjusting screw. Refer to the pattern sheet for diagrams of the processes described below.

Note: *When first using the large hoop after you have turned on the machine you need to place the hoop in the machine after the pattern is selected. You do not need to remove the hoop when selecting designs to be joined.*

There are two designs on Victorian Lace that can be embroidered using the large hoop—Lace 15a and b and Lace 20a and b. To position the large, joined-up piece you start with print out templates of each of the sections, overlaid and stuck together to make a whole design. Then determine the center of the large design. Note that the center of either of these large designs should be used to center the finished design but the center of each section of the design needs to be determined for actual stitching.

—Place the self-adhesive tear-away in the large hoop with the protective paper uppermost. Score around the inside edge of the hoop with a pin, then remove the protective coating.

FOR LACE 15A AND 15B
—select first part of the design and rotate it 180° to stitch the design right way up, then move the design 12 spaces to the left close to the center of the hoop.

NOTE: *Because Lace15a has too many stitches to fit in one memory it is divided between two—remember to sew the second part (file 2 of Lace15a) before moving onto lace 15b to complete the embroidery design.*

—place the hoop in the machine then slide the hoop down to stitch in the top section of the hoop first and tighten the adjusting screw

—place the center marked position for the first section of the design 15a on the fabric under the needle making sure the fabric is on the self-adhesive tear-away flat and straight, both vertically and horizontally

—stitch color No. 1 which are placement lines which should align with those drawn on the fabric

—embroider first file of the design 15a (remembering there is a second file which has to be stitched to complete the first half of the design 15a)

—to complete the second file of 15a, select file 2 of 15a, rotate the design 180° then move it 12 spaces to the left and stitch out file 2

—when the above design is complete (both files of 15a) use the fabric marking pen to mark the position of the last stitch in the design. This stitch is used as the starting position for the second half of the design (15b)

—select design 15b rotate it 180° then move it to the left 12 spaces to align with 15a

—go to color 2, press pattern start to get the needle centered in the starting position of the embroidery design

—release the screw at the side of the hoop to slide the hoop until the needle is exactly over the center starting position marked on the fabric—last stitch of 15a file2

—tighten the screw at the side of the hoop to secure it in place—this is very important and is often forgotten with disastrous results

—complete the embroidery design by manually advancing the colors (when the color is completed, press OK and Number 8 to advance to the next color). Do not forget to manually advance to the next color or you will restitch over this color again. When the design is complete remove fabric from the self-adhesive tear-away and press.

FOR LACE20A AND 20B

PLEASE NOTE: *If you wish to center this design (Lace20a and Lace20b as one motif) and not do it as a continuous connecting design, then you will need to use your software and delete the connecting bar at the end (top) of Lace20b. This should then be saved for a single pattern of Lace20a and Lace 20b rather than a continuous pattern of the two designs.*

—select Lace20a **DO NOT ROTATE THE DESIGN WHICH WILL BE STITCHED IN THE REAR END OF THE HOOP FIRST**, this defaults to a size 80 hoop, press top arrow key to the right to change the screen, then press '0' to default to 120 hoop. Move the design 13 spaces to the left to center the design in the hoop. Place the hoop in the machine and release the screw to move the hoop up to position the first part of the design in the rear of the hoop. Remember to tighten the adjusting screw when hoop is in position.

—place fabric on the hoop (design is stitched from the bottom to the top) so the needle sits exactly over the center marked position to stitch out the first section of the design (which appears up side down). Use fabric marking pen to mark the position of the last stitch

—select 20b, move the design 13 spaces to the left to center the hoop

NOTE: *Lace20b has too many stitches to fit in one memory so will be divided into two files—do not forget to sew the second part of lace20b (file 2) before removing the fabric from the hoop when the design is completed.*

—go to color 2 and press pattern start to reposition the needle in the starting position which aligns with the finishing stitch from 20a

—loosen the adjusting screw to slide the hoop until the needle sits exactly over the last stitch in 20a

—**TIGHTEN THE ADJUSTING SCREW AT THE SIDE OF THE HOOP TO SECURE IT IN PLACE—THIS IS VERY IMPORTANT AND IS OFTEN FORGOTTEN WITH DISASTROUS RESULTS**

—complete embroidery remembering to advance color manually as with 15b. Do not forget to advance to the next color remembering to complete all the embroidery design 20b file 1 and 20b file 2 before removing the hoop from the machine and the fabric from the hoop then pressing the design.

NOTE: *The above instructions are for the lace designs on the Victorian Lace CD that use the large hoop and may vary from other Pfaff cards that need the large hoop to stitch out designs. Other brands of machine will stitch these out in different ways.*

Credits

Pfaff Sales & Marketing
610 Winters Avenue, Paramus, NJ, 07652
Phone: 201 262 7221 Fax: 201 262 0696

JENNY HASKINS DESIGNS AVAILABLE FROM:
Pfaff Service: 31000 Viking Parkway
Westlake, OH 44145 Tel.: 1-800-356-1305
All Jenny Haskins Design CDs, Victorian Lace CD,
Victorian Pansies and Victorian Roses books

Unique Creative Opportunities Pty Limited
PO Box 2156 Carlingford NSW 2154 Australia
Phone/Fax 61 2 9680 1381
Email: jenny@rpi.net.au
Web site: **www.jennyhaskins.com**

Design Disks: *Victorian Roses, Victorian Pansies,
Victorian Scrolls and Curlicues, Victorian Bows and
Baskets, Victorian Butterflies Signature Disk, Victorian
Script and Frames, Victorian Patchworks Quilt Designs
and Victorian Cutwork tablecloth*

Fabric Prints and Accessories: *Victorian Silk Panels,
Victorian hand painted laces, Victorian beads, flowers
and fabrics*

USA Distributors of Jenny Haskins Products
Pollards Sew Creative
1934 E Alosta Avenue, Glendora CA 91740 USA
Phone 1 626 335 2770 Fax 1 626 335 4960
Email: pollards@pollardsewcreative.com
Web site: www.pollardsewcreative.com

Quilters' Resource Inc
Distributor of all Jenny Haskins books and CDs
PO Box 148850, Chicago, Il 60614
phone 1 773 278 5695 fax 1 773 278 1348
Email: info@ quiltersresource.com

Gloria Mckinnon and the team from
Anne's Glory Box produce unique creations with
fabric, thread and lace. For kits for projects on pages
94 to 97 contact Gloria on phone 61 2 4961 6016
fax 61 2 4961 6587
web site www.textiletraders.com.au/agb
email annesglorybox@bigpond.com.au
mail Anne's Glory Box, 60 Beaumont
Street, Hamilton NSW 2303
Australia

Wendy Fenwick is an award
winning doll maker, having
won Best of Show recently
with her latest creation,
Mr. Johann Sebastian Frog
(right) which was inspired
by a class with Betts Vidal.
She is a talented artist
whose palette of cloth and
thread leads her in many
creative directions. Bethany,
page 44, was made by Wendy
and is available in a kit form
for those who just have to replicate
her wonderful project. Contact
Wendy at: Kalyan Designs, 5 Mt
Pleasant Ave, Mona Vale NSW 2103 Australia. Email
fenwicks@attglobal.net

Sharman's Sewing Centers at Longview and Tyler
Texas, are owned by Sharman and Richard Dorsey
who are renowned for their special ways which
extend far beyond the boundaries of business. Each
store is a textile artist's Aladdin's cave, enticing the
eye and tempting the soul. The
staff excel in all areas of
creative stitching including
quilting, machine
embroidery and textile art,
running classes that always
have a waiting list. Both centers sell all the

products and tools needed to create the wonderful projects in Victorian Splendor including Pfaff sewing machines and accessories, and notions. The trousseau of lace trimmed linen on page 64 was created by the Sharman staff.
Contact Sharman on phone 1 903-753-8014 or Email Sharmans@aol.com.

The fabric in the background for photos on pages 45 and 46 the fabric frames for pages 100 and 101 are from **Yua Shoten** 2-5-4-Kawaramachi, Chuo-Ku Osaka 541-0048 Japan
Email: yuwa@yuwafabrics.com
Website: www.yuwafabrics.com

Delia Clough of Rosarium is an accomplished artist specializing in finely made jewelry and collectibles. She made the fans on page 31 and the masks on page 33.
Contact Delia on phone 61 8 9293 1457
fax 61 8 9293 0450
web site www.rosarium-deliaclough.com

Carole Cree, from Flights of Fancy brings to the 21st century all the charm and grace of the Victorian era. Carole, well known at craft shows where her work is much sought after, has been featured in Victoria, the benchmark magazine for Victoriana enthusiasts. Carole's love of beautiful hand embellishment techniques speaks for itself and her embellished prints which are available in kits are on page 99.
Contact Carole on phone 1 817 491 4681
Email: cjcreejr@earthlink.net

Lucienne Magnay, talent *extraordinaire*, is the maker of Splendor in Linen and Lace, page 70 and her gifts speak for themselves. **Elaine Pollard** is the other half of my brain and she patiently test sews my new ideas and stitch designs. To my friends, colleagues and guiding lights who I cannot do without—thank-you for all you do and say, and especially what you do not say; you make my days brighter, my heart lighter and my life happier.

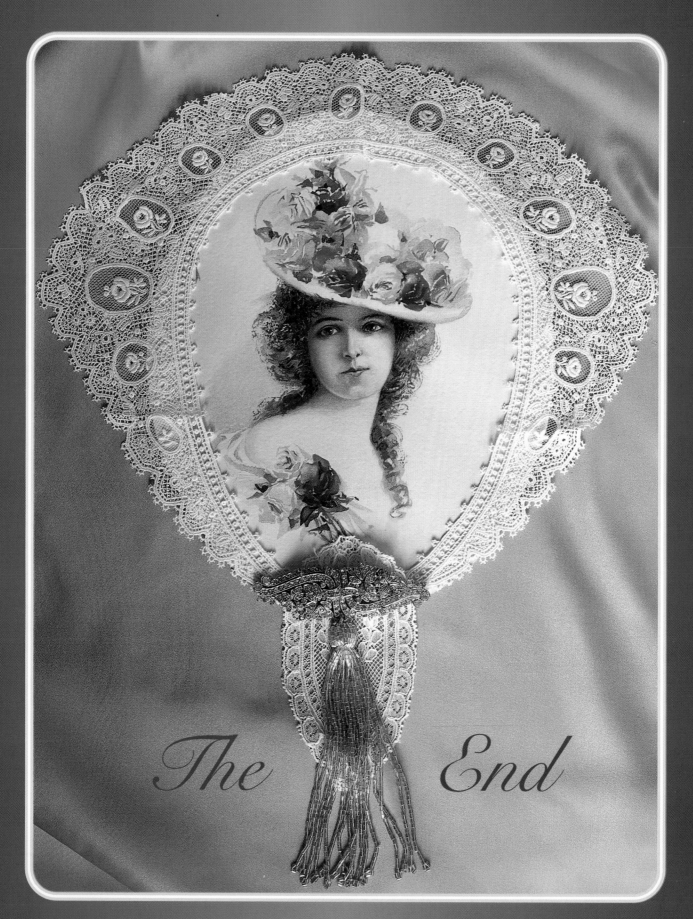

The *End*